The Kingdom Of God Triumphant

The Kingdom
Of God Triumphant

Allan Jellett

Go *publications*

Go Publications
Gibb Hill Farm, Ponsonby, Cumbria, CA20 1BX, ENGLAND

© Go Publications 2017

British Library Cataloguing in Publication Data available

ISBN 978-1-908475-10-7

Printed and bound in Great Britain
By Lightning Source UK Ltd.

Dedication

To my wife, Christine, and to my sons
who have helped and encouraged me
in the faith on our journey together
out of the error of religion into
the true gospel
'simplicity that is in Christ Jesus'
(2 Corinthians 11:3)

Contents

Preface

Between September 2015 and April 2016 I preached 27 sermons on the book of Revelation. Our church is a very small group of believers in Knebworth, England, about 25 miles north of central London, though we actually now meet in Welwyn Garden City about 4 miles from Knebworth. Our services are recorded and put on our website (www.knebworthgracechurch.org) and the sermons are uploaded to Sermon Audio, where they are accessible via www.freegraceradio.com. As a result we have a much bigger 'internet congregation' than the little group that gathers on a Sunday morning, and many people write to me regularly. I was asked frequently if I had considered writing up the sermons in the form of a book and finally I have bowed to the requests.

This is not another commentary on Revelation; I feel in no way qualified to undertake such a work. It is just my sermon notes expanded into the type of discourse I would have given as my sermons on Revelation. Each sermon can still be listened to on Sermon Audio and what is written in these chapters will be readily seen to be far from a transcription of those sermons. Nevertheless, I hope that what is written will come across in reading as sermonic in style and reasonably close to what was actually said when the sermons were first preached.

My basic position on Revelation for over 40 years has been a-millennial in interpretation; the vast bulk of the book is to be taken as symbolical rather than literal and I strongly believe that the a-millennial standpoint is consistent with the rest of scripture and the revelation of the gospel of grace throughout the scriptures. As a younger man I had been exposed to bizarre views arising from pre- and post-millennial teachings that, for example, saw Christ returning to reign for a literal 1,000 years in a literal Jerusalem over a world still in its sin with temple sacrifices restored. I found this literally incredible and in its place I gladly received the teaching of Stuart Olyott at Belvedere Road Baptist Church in Liverpool in the early 1970s which he had based squarely on William Hendriksen's Revelation commentary, *More Than Conquerors*.

9

In preparing my sermons I was greatly helped by Don Fortner's *Discovering Christ In Revelation*. His style is always very readable and his focus on Christ and his blessings on his people is unsurpassed. However, there are places in which readers might detect a divergence in my interpretation from Don's. That is largely because I was influenced, too, by the Revelation commentary of Herman Hoeksema, *Behold He Cometh*. Whilst I do not agree 100% with Hoeksema's interpretation, I find it very satisfying regarding the view he comes to of world history and God's rule over all things for his eternal purposes and the triumph of his kingdom over Satan's false kingdom.

At the time of writing this preface, some final additions to the chapters and the summary, I have no idea what will become of it all. I have no ambition for it other than to answer the requests of those who asked me to do it. It might remain as no more than a down-loadable link to a set of .pdf files. That is fine by me. If it is a blessing to anyone, I am more than happy.

Allan Jellett

Foreword

If there is one thing that enrages the world, and the religious world in particular, it is the fact of, the importance of, and the necessity of revelation in all true spiritual understanding. In the things of God, the things of eternity, we know nothing but what God reveals to us. In the things concerning Jesus Christ we know nothing, nothing at all, except God reveals Him to us. This book in the Bible, this prophecy of John's, reveals, makes known and sets forth, the Lord Jesus Christ as He really is throughout all time, and in eternity. It sets Him forth. It is the Revelation of Jesus Christ.

Now, whilst that is the name of the book, and whilst the book is a record by John of what God showed to him, for many people the allegories given do more to conceal than to reveal. In this we see the importance of God doing for us, what He did for John. God took John aside, alone on an island, alone on Patmos, and He revealed His Son to him. For you and me, if we are ever to see and to know Christ for who He really is, then God must also take us aside, alone with Himself, and reveal His Son to us. He will use this book in the Bible, The Revelation of Jesus Christ, but until He opens Him up to us in the Gospel, then Christ will remain concealed from our gaze.

My friend and brother, Allan Jellett, has presented us here with some rich insights, some glorious glimpses into what is found within John's prophecy. These, I am sure, will prove a great blessing to the hearts and souls of God's children. But again, God must take these words, this exposition, and open them up to you in particular. From the opening vision to the last words of the book, Christ is, and must be, revealed.

John opens the first chapter of this book by telling us of the tremendous vision of his ascended Lord and Saviour, which he saw, whilst on Patmos, whilst in the Spirit on the Lord's day. Here, the spiritual and allegorical nature of the book commences. Hid from the wise and prudent, yet revealed unto babes, we note in both the location

11

and the time, where, when, and from whence, Christ makes Himself known unto His own. In that spiritual day in which the Sun of Righteousness having risen with healing in His wings reigns on high above, shining forth His glorious light, having completed His great victorious work at the cross, and before His return in judgment at the end of time, in that day of the gospel, the Lord's day, Christ by His Spirit took His servant John and placed him in exile upon an island – away from the world, away from man, away from religion, away from everything, in order to reveal to him His glory. Then, and not until then, John saw.

Have you seen? Has the Lord Jesus placed you in your Patmos, away from everything, exiled from this world, all alone, but with Him?

Blessed is he that readeth, and they that hear the words of this prophecy, and keep those things which are written therein: for the time is at hand.

Revelation 1:3

Ian Potts

Chapter 1

Hidden Reality Revealed

Revelation 1:1-3

In June 2010 my wife and I flew to Geneva for a week's summer holiday walking in the mountains up above Montreux. From Geneva airport we took the train around the northern shore of Lake Geneva under grey skies and very limited views to the small town of Bex (pronounced Bay) at the eastern end of the lake, and from there we travelled by rack railway through the town and then up several thousand feet of extreme gradients into cloud and on to Villars. In Villars we walked down the main road from the station to our hotel in the chill of thick mist. It felt distinctly unlike summer.

The hotel reception was very pleasant, other guests were checking in and the whole atmosphere was friendly and welcoming. Our room was very comfortable and well-appointed, but from the balcony we could barely see the line of pine trees below us across the quiet road at the back of the hotel. The view was unrelenting grey.

Dinner was very good and we struck up a friendship with a couple of mature ladies who were sisters having a walking break away from their husbands. The next day was much the same; the pleasantries of the hotel, the meals, its staff and other guests continued, but the mist shrouded everything and limited our visibility to a few feet. Our experience of Switzerland was nothing like the promise of the brochures; had we known no better we would have reported that Switzerland has some very steep railways, some beautiful hotels, friendly people, but as far as scenery is concerned we would have said that it is uniformly grey with only the ghostly outlines of pine trees giving any relief.

The next morning we drew back the curtains and stepped out onto the balcony of our room into a glorious scene of snow-capped mountains bathed in brilliant sunshine. Thousands of feet below in the valley we

13

could see the upper part of the River Rhone and in the distance, Lake Geneva. Of course, it had been there all of the time but we just could not see it.

Often it seems like that in this world; we sense our immediate environment, the people with whom we come into contact, our daily routine with its highs and lows, health and sickness, times of plenty and times of shortage, births, marriages and deaths in the family and all of the world's events going on around us. There is as little sense of the things of eternity, and of God, heaven and hell, as we had of the glorious vista from our Swiss hotel balcony before the thick mist cleared. Yet, for those who have believed the gospel, God has granted faith, that sight of the soul, to see things unseen with natural eyes; the reality of it comes through the written Word of God with Holy Spirit guidance to give light so that we discern its truth and application. Paul writes to the Corinthians, in 1 Corinthians 2:14 that the natural man receiveth not the things of the Spirit of God ... for they are spiritually discerned, and in 2 Corinthians 4:18 that we look not at things which are seen, but things which are not seen: for the things which are seen are temporal; but the things which are not seen are eternal.

For New Testament Christians it has been like this since about AD 50, almost 2,000 years. We know God's Word promises an end of this sinful world and the dawn of a 'new heavens and a new earth' without any sinful defilement, but it feels like a very long wait and it still has not come to reality. How will God prevent his people from despairing? In about AD 95, God gave The Revelation of Jesus Christ to his church via the Apostle John.

First Century Situation
Imagine you are a believer living in the second half of the first century AD. Jesus Christ has been born, lived for 33 years, died the death of the cross. He has risen from the dead and ascended to heavenly glory witnessed by his apostles and many believers. The New Testament scriptures have been almost completed. The church has grown and spread around the Mediterranean Sea and the Roman world, in the face of persecution and violence. In AD 70 the Romans destroyed the temple at Jerusalem[1] and by the time we get beyond AD 90, all of the apostles have died, mostly violent deaths, and John[2] is over 90 years old and in exile on the Isle of Patmos in the Aegean sea between Greece and Turkey.

---

[1] Never to be reinstated to this day

[2] John, the 'beloved apostle', the writer of John's gospel and three epistles.

To the physical sense of believers, the scene appears as inspiring as, once again, our mist-shrouded arrival in the Swiss mountains. But to see things spiritually, to be comforted in their souls, we need to see beyond the mist to eternal realities from God's perspective. Therefore, for these first century believers and for us, through John's exile and physical deprivation on Patmos, God provides a 'spy-hole' through the thick mist of this fallen world into the glorious sunshine of God's eternal purposes.

Structure Of Revelation
From the very start it helps to keep in mind some key points about the structure and nature of the book of Revelation. First, it is a collection of visions and much of what is written is intended to be understood figuratively. Generally, it is clear where things should be taken literally, though the majority of the book is symbolical. The very first verse says that God 'sent and signified' the vision(s) by his angel unto his servant John. Signified clearly implies symbolism.

Secondly, it is vital not to mix literal and symbolic interpretation in the same vision. It is this error that has led to so much of the absurdly fantastical nonsense that has been written on Revelation from many quarters.

Thirdly, it is not chronological; the chapters do not form an historical sequence of events from chapter 1 through to chapter 22. This erroneous approach has also generated bizarre notions that are of no benefit at all to God's people.

Fourthly, it is likely that most of the terrible things seen, especially in the seals, trumpets and vials, apply to some extent throughout created time, or at least throughout the time since Christ's ascension, but that they undoubtedly increase in their intensity and severity as the end of time approaches. When we see the completion of the seven vials of wrath at the end of chapter 16, it is clearly the end of this space-time creation, and the end of history, though there are six more chapters to go before we reach the end of the book.

In fact, the book is a collection of seven distinct revelations, each covering either the whole of history from the Fall in Eden to the end of world time, or from the time of Christ's first coming to his second coming. Each one provides a different perspective on the same eternal plan of God, which plan involves the restoration of his unrivalled rule over all things and the defeat of Satan and his demonic plans. Seven is the number of divine perfection or completeness, hence there are seven visions. We will see this number many times, and whilst we will only scratch the surface of biblical numerics and their significance, we will find convincing confirmation of the symbolical, visionary nature of the book in the numbers quoted. The seven visions can be summarised as follows:

Chapters 1-3

A view of the ascended, reigning, glorified Christ in the midst of his people, called his church in all its local manifestations in the world but separate from the world, throughout the time from his ascension to his return at the end of time. Basically, this reveals the praise, rebuke and exhortations of Christ to his people, the church, living in this fallen world as they bear witness of him and await his return.

Chapters 4-7

Christ opening and fulfilling the seven-sealed book of God's eternal plan to restore his rightful, unrivalled rule over all things by the defeat of Satan and his forces of evil rebellion, the seventh seal revealing itself in the third vision as seven trumpets.

Chapters 8-11

Christ protecting his praying people and providentially executing seven trumpets of judgment to frustrate Satan's intentions, the seventh of which is seen in the fifth vision in the seven vials of wrath.

Chapters 12-14

A history of the people of God, the church of the Old and New Testament which brings forth Christ for the purpose of redemption in this world persecuted by Satan and beset by false philosophy and religion.

Chapters 15-16

Christ sending angels to pour out seven vials of wrath, the just judgments of God against sin.

Chapters 17-19

The true identity and source of all false religion, its impact on world
history, and its final destruction along with the beast and the false
prophet.

Chapters 20-22

Satan's final downfall and the glory of the New Jerusalem.

The book concludes with an epilogue and a gospel call to come and
drink of the water of life freely.

The Revelation Of Jesus Christ
The book of Revelation was written by the apostle John but it is the
Revelation of Jesus Christ. He who is God was made man; he came in
the flesh to redeem his people, and it is he who was given this Revelation
by God in his office as the God-man mediator (1 Timothy 2:5). John has
previously told us that Jesus Christ is the manifestation of the truth of
God to his people, 'No man hath seen God at any time; the only begotten
Son, which is in the bosom of the Father, he hath declared him' (John
1:18). If you would know God, you must have Jesus Christ, in all his
divine offices of mediation, revealed to you and in you (John 14:9;
Galatians 1:16). He is the message of scripture to the people the Father
chose in him before time began. The purpose of the Bible is not to teach
all men how God wants them to live as so many falsely claim; rather it is
God's message to his people of salvation from just condemnation,
accomplished by Christ, his people's Substitute. Christ himself told the
Pharisees that the overriding purpose of the Old Testament scriptures was
to testify of him (John 5:39); when he rose from the dead he expounded
to his disciples in all the Old Testament the things concerning himself
(Luke 24).
Paul could say to the Ephesian church elders (Acts 20:27) without
fear of contradiction that he had declared the 'whole counsel of God'
wherever he had been and, what is that whole counsel of God if it is not
what he wrote in 1 Corinthians 2:2, namely, Jesus Christ and him
crucified? If you would know peace with God you must know that you

17

are in Christ who has redeemed you from the curse of the law (Galatians 3:13) and that knowledge comes by believing (Romans 15:13).

Just as in the rest of the scriptures, so here in Revelation, the subject and the focus of the entire book is the Lord Jesus Christ and his accomplishments. It is the establishment of the kingdom of God by Christ. The salvation, redemption, preparation and qualification of the kingdom's citizens, chosen before the foundation of the world, whom the Father gave to Christ to make fit, despite their having fallen in Adam, for the presence of God (Ephesians 1:4). All who miss this in their desperation to fit everything in the visions and into what they see as a coherent view of the end of things, completely miss the point of the book.

Shown To His Servants

The first verse of Revelation tells us that God gave the Revelation to Jesus Christ with the express purpose of showing to his servants things which must shortly come to pass. The way his servants see what he shows them is by and through the visions, the symbolism signified by his angel or messenger to the apostle John, who is also a servant. It is not as though God gazed into a divine 'crystal ball' to see the future, rather it is that he as God, sovereign and omnipotent over all things, has ordained the things that must shortly come to pass. He reveals the future because he has determined the future and by virtue of his nature as God, it must all come to pass as he ordained. Believers can take great comfort from that knowledge; nothing happens that is out of the direct control of the God of the universe but all things are planned for the eternal good of his chosen people (Romans 8:28).

We might ask, "Why did God choose to reveal these things to his servants?" "Could he not have saved his people and taken them to eternal glory without them needing to know the details?" Yes, he could have, yet it is in the nature of God to reveal his truth to his saints. 'He sheweth his word unto Jacob' (Psalm 147:19). It is his will that his believing people should know what he has decreed when the unbelieving world in all ages languishes in spiritual darkness. Jesus told his disciples that they were his friends (John 15:15) and therefore he has shared with them the secrets of the triune God. Furthermore, the Word of God, and the mystery of the gospel of redeeming grace it reveals, is made clear only to the saints of God (Colossians 1:26). Has he shown it to you? Has he given you heart-faith to believe willingly the truth of sin, judgment, justice and the satisfaction made for his elect by the doing and dying of Christ? Has he given you a measure of the spiritual discernment that is exclusive to those enlightened by his Spirit? (1 Corinthians 2:6-16).

18

Sent By His Angel To John Who Bare Record

There is a pattern to the way God imparts his truth to his people; one shows it to another, who in turn shows it to another, and so on (2 Timothy 2:2). He uses angels to communicate his truths, messengers of the sinless, heavenly kind as in times past, or human messengers; prophets, apostles, pastors, evangelists and teachers (Ephesians 4:11). These pass on his message, even though in the case of the human 'angels' they constitute but earthen vessels (2 Corinthians 4:7); fragile, breakable, sinful men.

Nor does God need the platforms and methods considered essential by today's communicators; marketing and public relations, though he uses whatever means he will. It is noticeable that many of the New Testament epistles of Paul were written from prison or other situations where the writer was deprived of liberty and comfortable facilities, yet what a blessing we have as a result in our Bibles today. John, too, was exiled to Patmos, not given a public platform in Athens or Rome, that we might be given the Revelation. Much more recently, John Bunyan was confined to Bedford jail for twelve years where he wrote *Pilgrim's Progress* and other books that have spoken powerfully to many through the years. This is God's way of ensuring that flesh does not get the glory for his message. He uses things that seem inappropriate and ineffective to confound the wisdom of the world (1 Corinthians 1:18-25).

And so we have the book of Revelation in our hands. Do you understand it? Probably you will confess readily that you struggle with it. Yet, we can confidently expect that together with the message God has also given true spiritual light to his servants who are able to open it to others. I count myself as one who very much needs the help of others whom God has gifted to open these visions, and with his Spirit's help we trust that we will be given appropriate light as we proceed.

With The Intention Of Blessing His Servants

We are told in verse 3 that those who read, hear and keep the words of this prophecy of Revelation are blessed; we note it is not required that we understand everything. We are called to read and hear it (Hosea 4:1; Luke 8:18) praying for God's Spirit to guide and teach us. This is the spirit of the 'noble Bereans' (Acts 17:10, 11) who daily compared what they were hearing preached with what they read in the scriptures.

We are also told to keep the words of this prophecy. This cannot be a legal obedience in the flesh because the flesh is too weak. But I think it is exhorting us to build our life philosophy on these words, like the wise man in Jesus' parable (Matthew 7:24 ff.) who built his life on the words

19

of Christ. We may not understand all things perfectly, but with God's help we will see revealed amazing things concerning the eternal reality of our God, his sovereign control over all things for the eternal good of his people, and the excellent majesty of our Lord and Saviour, Jesus Christ.

Chapter 2

'Behold, he cometh ...'

Revelation 1

I remember, as a young child, having irrational night-time fears. I suppose fundamentally they were fears of the unknown; is there a monster in the wardrobe? If it is not in the wardrobe, surely, it is under the bed. I remember my own sons when they were young having similar fears and needing parental reassurance that there was no need to be afraid because, as their dad, I knew for certain there were no nasty monsters about to snatch them away. Only then, when fears were calmed, could they go to sleep reassured.

Believer, do you fear the unknown? We are surely living in 'perilous times' (2 Timothy 3:1). Are you anxious about the future? Does your world often feel as though it is filled with darkness? Opposition to the gospel of grace that you believe seems to increase with every day that passes. Distortion of the true gospel abounds. Perhaps you find yourself in a very lonely situation compelled to leave the church you once attended due to doctrinal and practical compromise with false religion and the world. You believe the gospel promises and you trust Christ for eternal life in heaven with God, but it is tempting to take your eyes off that glorious prospect and look down at the stormy waves of everyday life in this sinful world.

The book of Revelation is like the comforting visit of a parent to the fearful child in the night. It gives a glimpse into the clear day of God's eternity through the thick mist of mortal life and with this sight, believers are comforted and encouraged not to be afraid. Why? Because Christ, our sovereign, omnipotent God; Christ our master, friend and husband, is

21

both here among us and is coming again. He, who cannot lie, has promised that he is 'coming with clouds'.

The First Vision Of Revelation

Chapters 1-3 of Revelation contains the first of the seven visions of the book. It is a vision of the church of Christ. Here we see his true, believing people in their local churches, living in this fallen world and seeking to serve their Lord until he returns to establish his unrivalled kingdom. But above all it is a vision of who Christ is, where he is now, and what he is doing while the church lives in these last days of this New Testament dispensation. From this vision, fearful, misunderstood, persecuted believers can take immense comfort. Chapters 1-3 of Revelation is also rich with direct instruction, praise and rebuke to the churches concerning how they are to live in this world though in 'wilderness separation' from it. We note in passing that such direct instruction as is given to the seven real but also symbolical churches in chapters 2 and 3, contains nothing concerning keeping the law of Moses or what so many falsely teach today about the believer's obligation to Moses' law as their 'rule of life', but more of that later.

The vision is given by Christ to his servants via the apostle John who in verse 9 describes himself simply as the 'brother' of all true believers, and their companion in tribulation. Note, there is no hint of any hierarchy or levels of superiority in God's true church. John, the last surviving apostle, is conscious that he is but a sinner saved by grace. The focus of attention is Christ, the ascended, glorified Christ, and him alone.

Who Is Christ?

The more we know Christ, the more we are happy to rest in the assurance of his sovereign omnipotence. For many years I worked in business project management and I learned by experience that it was vital to get senior management 'on-board' with the project as early in the process as possible. They needed to understand the project's objectives, and I needed them to enable me to deliver those objectives successfully. They were the people with the power to make necessary things happen. Believer, come and see who is 'on your side' in this world.

In verses 4-7 the Lord Jesus Christ sends grace and peace to his churches. Here are God's chosen people who demonstrate their election by their belief of the truth (2 Thessalonians 2:13). Verse 4 tells us that the Saviour is revealed, or is ministered, to his people through the seven Spirits which are before his throne. There is but one Holy Spirit of God but this is saying that our Saviour is experienced by God's believing

22

people in the perfection, indicated by the number seven, of his ministration. God does not send anger, wrath, or condemnation to his people. True, there are times when a word of rebuke is needed as we shall see in chapters 2 and 3, but the overriding message of God to his people is 'comfort' (Isaiah 40:1). I might wish you well, others tell us to 'have a nice day', but none of us have more than the feeblest ability to affect outcomes. However, our great God, in Christ, has absolute control over everything that happens in this world. He does indeed cause all things to work together for good to his people (Romans 8:28).

Jesus Christ as we see him here in Revelation 1 is no longer in the state of his earthly humility. He is ascended. He is victorious over the powers of darkness. He is restored to the glory that he had with the Father before the world was (John 17:5). The fulness of the godhead dwelt in him on earth but it was veiled from most. Now in heaven he is the 'express image' of the person of God (Hebrews 1:1-3). He is the faithful witness of the truth of God, the very Word of God (Revelation 19:13). He is victorious in his accomplished redemption having satisfied divine justice as his people's Substitute. This is God who became man to redeem man (Philippians 2:5-11). This is infinite God 'contracted to a span' as the hymn-writer put it. He was tempted as man but remained sinless proving him a worthy Passover Lamb (1 Corinthians 5:7). He was made the sin of his covenant people at Calvary (2 Corinthians 5:21). He was judged guilty of sin and bore the just penalty of it in his death so that divine justice is now satisfied in respect of everyone for whom Christ died (Revelation 1:5, 6). In him, in Christ, mercy and truth met without contradiction, and righteousness and peace have kissed (Psalm 85:10). By his redemption our great God is indeed a just God and a Saviour, he remains perfectly just and yet in complete conformity to his righteous nature and by Christ's death he is able to justify his people (Isaiah 45:21; Romans 3:26).

The Lord Jesus Christ is the manifestation of the unknowable God to those who believe (John 1:1, 14, 18). It is through him, through believing in him that 'ye might have life through his name' (John 20:31). The vision of him that John records in Revelation 1 accords closely with the visions given to Daniel (chapters 7 and 10 especially). He appears and speaks as the Ancient of Days (Daniel 7:9), the eternal God, the Alpha and Omega, the first and the last, and he speaks words of peace and comfort to his people. Every aspect of the symbolism in the vision that John sees speaks of Christ's unrivalled ability to accomplish everything

23

he has decreed. Believer, you may feel so small and insignificant but God in Christ is ruling the universe and he is on your side!

Where Is Christ Now?

Verse 13 tells us that Christ, the Son of Man, the God-man mediator and redeemer, is in the midst of the seven candlesticks. Candlesticks are intended to hold candles, and candles give light. Verse 20 tells us that the candlesticks are the seven churches whereby we see it is the churches of God in this dark world who hold the light given by God. The light they hold is the gospel light of Christ, salvation light, the light of the knowledge of the glory of God in the face of Jesus Christ (2 Corinthians 4:6). The mission of the church of Christ is not to preach to people how God wants them to live, it is to declare the gospel of accomplished salvation in Christ, it is to share Paul's determination to know nothing other than Jesus Christ and him crucified. That is what it is to preach the 'whole counsel of God' (1 Corinthians 2:2; Acts 20:27). If we are his true people, gathered in a local church[3], we are one of his 'seven candlesticks' whose purpose is to bear his light.

The seven churches were real, literal, historical, geographically-placed churches in the time that John wrote; they are listed by name and chapters 2 and 3 contain dictated letters from our glorious Christ to each one of them individually in their real situation. But at the same time, seven is God's number of perfection or divine completeness. Thus, though literal historical churches, these seven congregations are also symbolical of the whole church of Christ in this world from the time of Christ's ascension until his return at the end of time. The letters are to all true churches of Christ throughout this AD time period. Thus we can say with confidence that he is here in the midst of all his churches today. Let me be clear, by this I mean his true churches, that is, those and those alone who confess that Jesus Christ is come in the flesh (1 John 4:1). That means they confess that he is the Messiah, the promised Messiah of the Old Testament, the One commissioned by sovereign electing grace for the redemption of his people. Perhaps you know little about being in a church fellowship. Perhaps you are on your own as a believer. Here is a gospel promise for you: God has promised to set the solitary in families (Psalm 68:8). What a blessing it is in these days that many solitary believers are finding true gospel fellowship online!

Fearful little flock of Christ; do not be anxious for anything, the Sovereign of the universe is here in the midst of his churches. This world

---

[3] Even if that is by the internet for solitary believers in these days.

may often seem like 'the valley of the shadow of death' but we need fear
no evil for our God is with his people (Psalm 23:4). Whether we are in a
significant assembly of God's saints, or worshipping with two or three
other believers, or even alone, our God is in our midst. He promises many
times in scripture to be our God and for us to be his people. Knowing this
we can trust him and live unafraid of what man can do (Psalm 56:11).

What Is Christ Doing?

Verse 7 calls for our attention, 'Behold'! Look now! He is in the process
of coming again and coming finally to bring to an end all things of this
space-time creation. He is not slack concerning his promise (2 Peter 3:8,
9). All things, all history, all world politics and natural processes are
moving unstoppably to their climax when Christ our glorious God comes
again. We are told that he comes with clouds. This speaks of the glory of
God (Psalm 97:2) as when he was veiled in cloud at his transfiguration,
and when he ascended and a cloud received him from the disciples' sight.
This second coming is not like the first coming of Christ which was in
humility for the purpose of salvation. Now he comes in glorious triumph
and dreadful judgment over Satan and the forces of evil. He shall come
not to redeem his people but to claim his redeemed possession and take
them to be with him forever. He shall come not to suffer the scorn and
spite of sinful men but to judge them in the righteousness of God.

We shall see in the remaining visions of Revelation the way in which
God is ordering all the affairs of this space-time creation to the ultimate
end of the triumphant coming of the Kingdom of God. Things are not just
happening randomly or erratically; God is ordaining everything to
frustrate Satan's evil purposes until the final and complete victory of
Jesus Christ.

When he comes, we read, 'every eye shall see him'. All who have
rejected him, scorned him, cursed him, violated his law and justice,
rebelled against his rightful rule, all of these shall see him with terror.
His people shall see him with unspeakable joy. When he returns it will
be not as the 'suffering servant' but as 'King of kings', not in humility
but in majesty. Indeed every knee shall bow to him (Isaiah 45:22-24;
Philippians 2:9-11). You who have rejected his word and his rule will
bow the knee in utter dread and regret and confess that he is Lord. A
storm of judgment is coming and Christ is the only refuge (Isaiah 32:2).

Now, today, he says to all who are burdened with the guilt of sin, who
know the justice of God in condemning sin, who know they deserve
eternal condemnation, he says to them, and perhaps therefore to you,

'come unto me ... and I will give you rest for your souls'. Can you heed the warnings? Do you hear the gospel call?

For you who believe, will you seek God's help to live in the light of this knowledge that he is, even now, in the process of coming? Paul wrote to Titus in Titus 2:13 about 'looking for the blessed hope and glorious appearing of the great God and our Saviour Jesus Christ.' What expectation, hope and joy this should cause in those who believe. Surely I come quickly Amen, even so come Lord Jesus (Revelation 22:20).

Chapter 3

Letters For Today's Local Churches

Revelation 2 and 3

Arriving at these two chapters of Revelation, I was aware it had not been long since I preached a series of messages on the letters to the seven churches to our own little church fellowship and so, rather than repeat much of that material, it seemed appropriate to try to condense the two chapters into one message[4].

We are in the first of the seven visions of the book of Revelation and this first vision occupies Revelation chapters 1 to 3. Whilst the seven churches were real historical churches in what we now know as western Turkey, they are representative of every local church throughout the world in this time period from Christ's ascension to his glorious return at the end of time. The letters speak to us now. They are personally dictated by the Lord Jesus Christ to John to send to the churches, and as such, are the words of the living, glorified Christ to us in our local churches today. They do not constitute, as some falsely teach, an allegory of the development of the church down the ages since the first century AD. To argue this is as unprofitable as arguing about genealogies and the like (Titus 3:9).

The way to view this vision and handle the messages to the churches it contains is with the same anticipation as when an expected and vital letter arrives through the post. Are you ready to open the letter? The postman has just delivered it. Let us ask three simple questions; who is it from, who is it to and what does it say?

From The Living Christ
In Revelation 1:18 Christ tells us, 'I am he that liveth'. In Revelation 2:1 he tells us that he walks in the midst of the seven golden candlesticks,

---

[4] For any who would like a more detailed study, Don Fortner's book, *Discovering Christ In Revelation* provides a clear and detailed outline.

and verse 20 of chapter 1 tells us that these candlesticks are the seven churches, and therefore, all true churches in the period from his ascension to his final return. Thus it includes believers today. This is our God, the living Lord Jesus Christ, writing to us today and assuring us that he 'walks amongst us'. The teaching of some now-dead historical character, as interesting as such teaching might be, is the only aspect of them that lives on. But with Christ, he is alive today, speaking these words to us as he, by his Spirit, moves among us. The Holy Spirit of God takes the things of Christ and reveals them to his saints (Colossians 1:26). It is only by divine revelation that the things of God are discerned because flesh, and the natural man without the life of God in his soul, is completely unable to discern these things irrespective of how worldly wise and intelligent it might otherwise be (1 Corinthians 2:14).

In the light of that reality, ask yourself if you ever received a more important letter from a more important person.

To All His Churches
Our living Lord Jesus Christ speaks to all his people and all his churches in all ages including us here and now. He is speaking to his own, among whom he moves right now in every condition and situation in which they find themselves during this extended period from his ascension to his return. If we are his then these letters are to us for they are addressed to all true believers. He describes these people in four ways.

First, these people have an ear to hear (Revelation 2:7, 11, 17, 29; 3:6, 13, 22). In our natural, physical state, in our flesh without the life of God in the soul, we do not have such an ear to hear. This spiritual hearing is the gift of God (Ephesians 2:8). He is sovereign over all things whether the natural man likes it or not; he is God and he is gracious to whom he will be gracious. If you have ears to hear what God says to his people then you are blessed indeed (Matthew 13:16). The gospel is a mystery to man in his natural, fleshy state but by grace God reveals it to his saints, whom he has set apart in Christ before the foundation of the world (Colossians 1:26; Ephesians 1:4).

Secondly, these people 'overcome' (Revelation 2:7, 11, 17, 26; 3:5, 12, 21). What do they 'overcome'? They overcome every temptation to give up following Christ by faith. They persevere. It is not in their own strength that they persevere but by Christ's keeping of his own dear people (John 10:29). Only those who have been truly born again of the Spirit of God will endure to the end and this they will do most certainly. When tempted to 'go away' their response is that of Peter (John 6:68), 'to whom shall we go, you have the words of eternal life'.

Thirdly, these people do not embrace false doctrine and the 'depths of Satan' (Revelation 2:24) yet they are not 'super saints'. They are far from perfect, nevertheless, they are not happily settled in Satan's lies; his false doctrine of 'heavenly' attainment by man's own efforts. All around us we see manmade religion calling itself 'Christianity' but teaching nothing other than the falsehood of Satan. We shall see in later chapters of Revelation how this false doctrine of Satan has manifested itself in world history and continues to do so today.

Fourthly, they are the people Christ loves and cares for (Revelation 3:19, 20). The Lord Jesus Christ loves all his people, all those who have been committed into his care by the eternal, electing love of God the Father. Some who are included in this care are like the Laodiceans, who were so full of their own material riches they had become lukewarm to the love of Christ. And some who, like the Prodigal Son, are far from living a 'credible testimony' of true faith yet knowing deep down whose they are and to whom they must return. These are they whom he rebukes with his fatherly chastisement; who hear his call and open the door that he might come in and sup with them.

The Lord does not write to the world, to people in general; he writes to his saints, his elect who have believed the gospel of sovereign grace and particular redemption. He tells them he knows every detail of their condition, he commends some things, he warns against others, he exhorts and encourages and he promises an eternal prize.

He Knows

The glorified Lord Jesus Christ, our God-man Redeemer, speaks now from heaven and tells his churches, his believing people, his saints in this world, that he knows their works. He knows the situation, the trials and the efforts of his people in his service, then and now. The infinite, omnipotent, sovereign God even now, today, knows everything about our situation as we seek to maintain a witness to the truth of the gospel in this sin-corrupted world. Nothing is hidden from his view. Therefore we need to consider these letters, to the seven real, historical but symbolical churches, as personally relevant to us as we gather together to worship and hear his word preached, whether that be in large or small congregations, or as individual believers with little personal fellowship.

He Commends ...

What characteristics of the life of believers, of churches in this world, does our Lord Jesus Christ commend? He commends dedication to his cause, to the cause of his kingdom, evidenced by works arising from true faith in the heart. Half-heartedness has no place in the kingdom of Christ especially in these days when the battle-lines between the world and the truth of God are drawn ever more clearly. The church is in a 'wilderness'. The church is separated from the world, its philosophies and values, but it is dwelling in close proximity to the world in the place prepared of God for it (Revelation 12:6). This is a place of trials, hardship, loneliness and opposition but the place, nevertheless, of God's appointing, the place where Christ prayed the Father that we should be kept from the evil (John 17:15). And so Christ commends his people in this world when they demonstrate patience in the face of trials of providence and of spirit. He commends them when they are diligent to maintain correct doctrine and will not tolerate gospel error and the precepts that arise from it. Beware of any who teach that the flesh is so corrupt that the outworking of our faith in these bodies does not matter; Christ sees all and he commends the good.

He Warns Against ...

As you read the seven letters in chapters 2 and 3 it is clear that Christ warns his churches against things which, if tolerated and unchecked, will cause the church to wither and fail. These are not empty warnings as evidenced by countless buildings in our land that were once churches and chapels in which the true gospel was preached but where the light of gospel truth has long since been extinguished. The name Ichabod, meaning departed glory, could be justly fixed above the door because the glorious gospel of effectual redemption ceased to be the focus and message of the church. Six issues are raised for us to be on guard to avoid.

    1. Apostasy from the believer's 'first love' (Revelation 2:4). However correct and commendable we may be in outward forms of Christian behaviour and doctrine, our witness will shrivel and die without a continuance of the first thrill of gospel love. When a sinner comes under Holy Spirit conviction and despairs of all hope of acceptance with God by law-works, when Christ is first revealed to the convicted soul and the saving power of his redeeming blood is grasped, that soul overflows with love to Christ. That love must and will continue but fleshly negligence may cause it to fluctuate, as pictured throughout the Song of Solomon, yet it must always revive and continue. What is the remedy for this perilous condition? Christ calls for repentance and a remembrance of how sweet it was to embrace him in those early first rushes of heartfelt love. There is no better way of calling divine truth to remembrance than to heed the message of God's word; for example, in Colossians 3:1-4

believers are reminded of their eternal state by virtue of grace and accomplished salvation. The verses call for our affections to be set on these things. This involves meditation, prayer, and contemplating the riches so lovingly bequeathed by God on the people of his choice. Where there is a true experience of grace in the soul such contemplation will surely revive the flame of love for Christ.

2. Compromise with false doctrine (Revelation 2:14). The doctrine of Balaam is the doctrine of compromise with worldly religion. As a prophet, Balaam could speak only what God gave him to speak. His utterances, recorded in Numbers 22 to 24, are full of gospel truth that God's purpose to bless the people of his choice with full and free salvation is certain to be fulfilled. Yet Balaam was a false prophet and we read in Numbers 25 that he seduced Israel to commit sexual immorality with the daughters of Moab, and in so doing to commit spiritual adultery by participating in the idolatrous practices of Baal worship. The religion of Baal is the religion followed by the majority of what calls itself Christianity in our day. Some of it sounds orthodox, like Balaam's prophecies, but it involves compromise with falsehood. It denies sovereign grace and particular redemption which lies at the core of the 'offence of the gospel' (2 Corinthians 6:14-18). It appeals to the religious reason of fallen man and therefore the flesh embraces it. But it is sternly condemned by Christ.

3. Antinomianism (Revelation 2:15). The doctrine of the Nicolaitans was probably antinomianism; its proponents taught that because justification was accomplished by Christ without any contribution from a person's law-works, it was, consequently, irrelevant how believers actually lived. They were free to 'sin that grace may abound'. Now, while it is true that believers are in no way under the law, any who think they can commit immoral and sinful acts with impunity are greatly deceived. Flying in the face both of the precepts of God's law and revealed gospel truth is antinomian and the Bible is clear, such lawbreakers will not inherit eternal life (1 Corinthians 6:9, 10). It is no surprise then that Christ says he hates it. If you truly have the love of Christ in your heart, that love constrains your outward behaviour (2 Corinthians 5:14).

4. Tolerance of false teachers (Revelation 2:20). A church may be praised for its diligence and charitable service and yet be a place where false teachers are tolerated. To such Christ issues his rebuke. In Thyatira they were seemingly allowing a woman to preach and teach deception. Whether her seduction was to physical fornication, or more likely, to that which was spiritual in nature, its Satanic purpose was to draw believers

away from Christ. Tolerance of everyone, acceptance of all perversion, even within the church, is today portrayed as the only gracious behaviour from those who call themselves Christians; not so according to Christ. We must be welcoming to all and preach the gospel to all who will listen, but we must not tolerate any who peddle religious falsehood in pursuit of gathering increased numbers.

5. Hypocrisy and formalism (Revelation 3:1). Churches that were once true to Christ and his gospel can drift into lifeless orthodoxy and forms of ritualism. There are countless examples of this in our day. The elders of such churches transform into the 'pastor's henchmen' who see it as their role to maintain the church's traditions and crush honest questioning. They encourage 'faithfulness to the gospel' which is actually only faithfulness to their rigid, legalistic rule. Practice may be outwardly orthodox and correct in many ways but merely in form; for example, communion may be observed in strict adherence to an established practice yet there be little evidence of truly discerning the Lord's body in its observance. Christ warns in the strongest terms that such practice is indicative not of healthy spiritual life but of death.

6. Lukewarmness (Revelation 3:15, 16). The Laodiceans were typical of many established, so-called 'evangelical' churches in our day. They look and feel completely self-satisfied; they appear materially prosperous, middle class and intellectually superior. Who dare question their credentials as local churches of Christ? Here Christ himself not only questions but issues the severest of warnings. He calls them lukewarm, neither hot in his service nor cold in opposition, but smugly self-satisfied. Is there any hint of that with us? O Lord, examine us and show us our sin! Are we just Sunday-service followers of Christ? Do we like to retain the 'benefits' of church but keep the option of running with the world? Christ says that it is an unsustainable position and he even puts it as strongly as to say he will 'spew such out of his mouth'. Such assemblies consider themselves to be local manifestations of his true church but they make him sick and they will not be allowed to continue. But listen; there must be some who are his true people even in Laodicea for he counsels them to return to him; he rebukes and chastens those whom he loves. Can you hear his voice? Will you repent? He is knocking at the door; can you hear? Will you open to him? Do you yearn for the restoration of 'sweetheart love' and fellowship with your Saviour?

Exhortation And Promise
Throughout these letters which apply equally to us as believers and churches today, Christ exhorts his people to hear his voice, to repent of

sin, and to hold fast to the truth of the gospel. He calls us to be watchful and intolerant of error and falsehood, to expect and look for his return and to be utterly committed to him and his service (Revelation 3:18).

Life for believers in this world is not easy; the 'spirit' may be willing but we are constantly reminded of the weakness of the flesh. We live in this world and often find ourselves entirely at odds with its philosophy, values and practices. We might ask, as did the writer of Psalm 73, "Why bother?" As 1 Corinthians 15:19 puts it, 'If in this life only we have hope in Christ, we are of all men most miserable', but the believer's hope is not limited to this earthly life; we have the promise of eternity, and Christ underlines his promise of eternal bliss several times throughout these letters. In Revelation 2:7, he promises that his people will eat fruit from the tree of life in the midst of God's paradise. In Revelation 2:10 and 11, he promises a crown of life and escape from the second death. In Revelation 2:17, he promises Christ's hidden manna and a white stone of justification when his people are brought to his judgment seat. In Revelation 2:26-28, he assures us we shall reign with him. In Revelation 3:4, 5, he promises the garments of salvation in which we shall walk with God eternally. In Revelation 3:12 we are promised a permanent, eternal, presence in the new Jerusalem. In Revelation 3:21, the promise is of unending intimate fellowship and communion with God.

This is the end of the first of the seven visions of Revelation; it has revealed to God's saints in churches on this earth, throughout the time from his ascension to his return in judgment, that he is alive now and present with his people. He is watching, knowing, encouraging, rebuking, leading and assuring. Do you have ears to hear what he has said to his church here and now? If you do you are blessed indeed.

The Kingdom Of God Triumphant

Chapter 4

'Come up hither …'

Revelation 4

We have seen in the first three chapters of Revelation the glorified, living Christ interacting with his blood-bought people, within their churches, throughout the period from his ascension to his return in judgment at the end of time. He speaks to his people by his 'angels', the pastors and teachers he has given to his church (Ephesians 4:11) for their journey of wilderness separation from the world whilst yet living in the world. He is living and speaking now to us today who believe. He speaks words of praise, rebuke, warning, encouragement and promise.

But why should we trust what we read? Generally, we trust people and organisations because of their reputation for honesty and integrity and we trust the rule of law to provide protection from dishonesty and criminality. Well, here in the second vision of Revelation in chapters 4 to 7, Christ by his servant John gives us heavenly, eternal reasons to trust our God now. It is this God-given heavenly perspective that reassures believers to trust his word and promises concerning eternal life. It is so easy in the flesh to be lulled into thinking that the 'here and now' is all there is of substance. But, despite their seeming permanence, God's word assures us it is the physical things of time that are temporary (2 Corinthians 4:18) while the unseen things of eternity are those which endure eternally. Furthermore, those unseen things are not far from each of us (Acts 17:27, 28). By grace the thief on the cross next to Christ had his perspective changed in an instant, and with the gift of repentance and faith cried out to the Lord to be remembered in eternity. The gracious reply came straight from the God-man, 'certainly this day you shall be with me in Paradise'. He was transported from the vile, shameful, disgusting, cruel death of the cross, in physical agony of body, straight into the bliss of sinless, eternal, fellowship with God. This was the promise and this was his experience. Indeed the things of eternity are 'not far from each one of us'. But how do we get in there to see them?

The Door

A door was opened in heaven (Revelation 4:1). This bears resemblance to Ezekiel 1:1 where the heavens were opened and the prophet saw visions of God. John heard a voice loud and clear like a trumpet calling him to come up into heaven to be shown things which must take place. And because the purpose of the Revelation is to show his believing people, his servants, things which must 'shortly come to pass' (Revelation 1:1), we may safely take it that all believers are bidden, through the medium of the Revelation to come up into heaven to see for themselves the things shown to John. But, let us be clear, the call is only to God's servants. They are those who believe the gospel of God's Son, they are people who have come into God's kingdom by the one and only way which is Christ 'the door' (John 10:9). He is the only way (John 14:6). It is impossible to come except by him. By his death and shed blood he has qualified his redeemed people to come (Colossians 1:12). By satisfying God's offended justice he has opened a new and living way of approach for those the Father gave to him in sovereign election before the world began (2 Timothy 1:9).

Do not think, however, that you can come, have a look and then, if you like what you see, decide to trust Christ! Our only entitlement to come is as the redeemed of the Lord. This blessed condition is evidenced by the presence of living faith in Christ. Faith in Christ is given by God's Spirit, bestowed through the hearing of the gospel and confirmed in redeemed sinners by their being set apart in belief of the truth of the gospel (2 Thessalonians 2:13). What qualifies his people is Christ's blood (Hebrews 10:19, 20). He has indeed saved to the uttermost (Hebrews 7:25) those who come to God through the door which is Christ Jesus.

Only as the redeemed of the Lord will you be able to see the truth and the importance of the things shown to John. Do not think your intellect will help you (1 Corinthians 2:14). The mystery of God, his revelation of divine, eternal truth is specifically given only to his saints (Colossians 1:26). Without that divine calling and gift, the things you read in the book of Revelation will be but 'foolishness'. Yet, with the benefit of the gift of faith (Ephesians 2:8), the precious, spiritual insight of soul given by God's Spirit to all of his people, you will see what John saw. You will 'behold a throne … set in heaven, and one sat on the throne' (Revelation 4:2). You will see Christ in all his glory.

A Throne And The Sovereign
In the vision given to him John sees a throne and a sovereign ruler upon that throne. He sees one who rules. This is, of course, consistent with the testimony of scripture concerning the enthroned Son of God, for example in Psalm 93 and Psalm 97:1. The God of the Bible is the God of the universe, and as God he rules over all things absolutely.

In the following verses we are given similes of precious stones; jasper to represent the glorious perfections of God, sardine speaking of the blood-red of God's justice. Around the throne John saw a rainbow with the appearance of an emerald; these indicate God's covenant mercy to his elect people and perhaps the emerald suggests the green of budding nature and a new creation. In verse 5 we read of lightning and thunder indicating the terror and wrath of God in respect of sin. Then we read immediately of 'voices' succeeding the thunder and lightning, indicating God's mercy and grace in contrast to his holy wrath.

The seven lamps of fire burning before the throne indicate the seven-fold, that is, perfectly complete, proceeding of the Holy Spirit of God from the presence of God to comfort the people of God.

In verse 6 we read of a 'sea of glass'; this is suggestive of the water in the laver at the temple in Jerusalem where the priests were told to wash before undertaking the service of God in the sacrifices and service of the temple. This would seem to indicate cleansing in the blood of Christ for all who are brought into God's presence.

Believer, this is for your comfort. Our God reigns supreme in everything. In this world of turmoil, uncertainty and fragility of existence, God, the sinner's friend in Christ, controls all things to fulfil his own purpose. In contrast the world grasps at straws for comfort, rejoicing, for example, in finding new astronomical discoveries while with divinely gifted faith the people of God see God inhabiting eternity and ruling over all things in this created universe made by him and for him (Revelation 4:11). What is your paradigm of life? If you subscribe to the unbelieving world's view of random, causeless, evolutionary materialism then you, along with the rest of the world, will bend every observation to make it fit your paradigm without any need for God. But if you are a true believer in the Lord Jesus Christ with the gift of faith to see what John saw, you will see God, the beginning of all creation and the source of all sustaining providence. You will see him in complete control of all things pertaining to time and eternity and from it you will take immense comfort.

The Twenty-four Elders

In verse 4 we read of twenty-four elders sitting on seats around the throne. These symbolise the church of the Old and New Testaments in glory, outside of time. Though time-bound here and now in this world, believers are said to be sitting in heavenly places in Christ in eternity (Ephesians 2:6). In this space/time creation we are here upon the earth. But as believers we are in the world yet not of the world. The vision given to John is of eternity outside of time. He sees the complete number of the elect of God, what he later sees as a multitude which no man can number, and yet a specific, precise gathering of the elect of God; sanctified, justified and glorified. They are clothed in white which speaks of them being made the righteousness of God in Christ. These are the garments of salvation (Isaiah 61:10) with which God clothes his people. Does this sound a bit unreal? Remember, the things which we see here and now are the things which are temporary, the things John saw in his vision are eternal, fixed, unchanging, permanent, solid and reliable.

The Four Beasts

In verse 6, John sees four beasts. There is speculation as to what these beasts represent. Here again there is similarity to Ezekiel 1:5-14 where the prophet sees visions of the eternal kingdom, of God's kingdom supplanting Satan's. The number four is the Biblical number of creation and the physical world. The beasts appear as a lion, speaking of strength, a calf or a young ox, indicating hard work, a man which suggests intelligence, being unique among God's creatures and made in the image of God (Genesis 1:27), and an eagle renowned among creatures for wisdom and swiftness. It could be that this is indicating that this present creation, marred as it is by sin, will be replaced in eternity when God's unrivalled kingdom is established with a new creation as seen in the last vision of the book (Revelation 21:1). That is itself a comforting thought but I agree with Don Fortner that there is something more here.

If you read Revelation 5:8-10 the four beasts sing with the twenty-four elders praise to God for their redemption unto God. Yes, creation is redeemed from the curse of sin (Romans 8:19-22) and a new heavens and earth are brought in, but the four beasts are with the elders, whom we have seen represent the church throughout time, singing the song of redemption. It seems plausible that these are gospel preachers, together with Old Testament prophets, all in the midst of the throne of God doing his bidding and (v. 9) giving him glory. What is the chief glory of God? Is it not his sovereign grace (Exodus 33:18, 19)? How do the beasts give glory to God? By preaching to sinners the grace of God found in Christ.

Even the likenesses speak of true preachers and prophets. They are like lions, bold in the face of opposition. They are like oxen, or a calf, diligent in service to God. They have the empathy of men for their fellow-man; and, like eagles, they have wisdom from Christ who is all-wise, with swiftness and agility, in doing his work. These are the seven stars in the right hand of Christ as he walks among his churches (Revelation 1:20). They are his ministry gifts to his people in all ages to feed his church in its wilderness journey here in the world (Revelation 12:6). When the beasts give glory to God in the preaching of the gospel of his grace (Revelation 4:9) the elders worship (Revelation 4:10). What is it that promotes true worship in this world? It is not ornate buildings or mystical liturgies, it is not doctrine and legal precept, it is gospel preaching of salvation by Christ alone, for to preach Christ is to proclaim the whole counsel of God (1 Corinthians 2:2, Acts 20:27). Only such preaching draws the heart-felt response from God's saints of 'Thou art worthy' (Revelation 4:11).

Conclusion
As believers in this world, knowing we are in Christ and therefore on a solid foundation of accomplished salvation in him, it is easy to become distracted by the things of this world; our career, family, finances, home, etc.. This part of the Revelation says to us, 'come up hither and see things from God's eternal perspective'. Come through Christ, the door in heaven, and see who is in complete control of all things. See the church in its eternal abode, see all creation under his control. See it heading for the triumphal replacement of Satan's kingdom, and thank God for giving us gospel preachers to feed his people in this space/time sojourn.

The Kingdom Of God Triumphant

Chapter 5

'Thy kingdom come ...'

Revelation 5

In chapter 5 of Revelation the vision of chapter 4, the second of the seven visions of the whole book, continues. John has been summoned up to heaven through a door and he has seen at the centre of all things a throne and one sat upon it in supreme majesty. He has seen the Spirit of God manifested as seven lamps of fire burning before the throne indicating the perfection of his ministrations. There were twenty-four elders and four beasts, the former representing the complete church of the Old and New Testaments, 12 patriarchs and 12 apostles, with the latter possibly representing gospel preachers, but perhaps also representing creation as four is its number. Then in chapter 5 we are given more detail. We see a book, a challenge, a null response, a lion who is a lamb and a multitude praising the lamb. What can it all mean and what relevance does it have for us here and now as believers?

Think back to the earthly ministry of our Lord Jesus Christ. What was the message at the heart of his preaching? It was the kingdom of God; he announced that the kingdom of God was at hand and he called for repentance in preparation for its coming. When the disciples asked him to teach them to pray, a central petition of the prayer he taught them was, 'Thy kingdom come'. The message of the scriptures is that God is establishing his eternal kingdom, a kingdom of righteousness, peace, and blessedness without any sin. God's kingdom will overthrow and finally replace the kingdom of this world. The days of Satan's kingdom with its sin, defilement, rebellion against God and its lie of heavenly attainment without the satisfaction of divine justice, are numbered. Great voices sing in Revelation 11:15, and are echoed in the Hallelujah Chorus of Handel's oratorio, Messiah, 'The kingdoms of this world are become the kingdoms of our Lord, and of his Christ; and he shall reign for ever and ever.' So we, and all his true people, pray, 'Thy kingdom come!'

With that in mind, let us now look at Revelation chapter 5.

41

The Book

In God's right hand there is a book covered with writing indicating that there is no blank space where anything can be added. It is a book that is complete, that stands as a unity and must not be added to nor taken away from. The text actually says the book is on rather than in the right hand of God indicating God's hand is open and the book is being offered to another. It has seven seals signifying it is perfect, and divinely complete. But it is closed up such that it cannot be readily opened (v. 3). That it is the book of the purposes of God in establishing his kingdom is evident from verses 9 and 10. The book is God's plan to conquer Satan and all worldly rule and to establish his unrivalled kingdom of peace and righteousness. Anyone who has ever worked in business on a project will know it is essential to have a plan to accomplish the objectives of the project. All involved must know clearly what it is intended to achieve, how success will be measured and what is the inter-dependent sequence of work packages that must be undertaken on the way to completion. This book that John saw is God's plan for the achievement of his objective of overthrowing and destroying Satan's kingdom while establishing his own unrivalled kingdom in its place.

But the book is perfectly sealed (v. 7) and, as such, it cannot be implemented. If the plan is to be implemented its seals must be loosed and the book opened, looked on and read (vv. 3, 4). Loosing the seal does not only reveal the book's contents, it implements the plan. If God's kingdom is to come, this book's seals must be loosed.

The Challenge And The Response

John reports seeing a strong angel asking a question (v. 2). Angels are God's messengers, God's spokesmen, and this one is strong implying that his question is announced so loudly as to be heard by all creation. Angels, powers, principalities and men all hear it. The question is, 'Who is worthy to loose the book's seals?' By this he is asking who is capable, and qualified to implement God's plan and establish his kingdom of peace and righteousness. The challenge goes out to all. All worldly empires, human philosophy, science and technology, political systems of monarchy, democracy, theocracy and all worldly religions are challenged to step forward and fulfil God's plan of establishing his kingdom.

But there is no response to the challenge. All the attempts of men to establish a utopia of peace and heavenly attainment have, without exception, failed. From Nimrod and the Tower of Babel and all the world empires that followed: Babylon, Medo-Persia, Greece, Rome, the Holy

42

Roman Empire, European monarchies, Hitler and the Third Reich, the Soviet Union to modern, 21st Century democracies, and even Islamic State, not one has succeeded. They only bring death, destruction, exploitation and obscene extremes of wealth and poverty. Is it not clear how bankrupt is all hope of eternal blessing outside of Christ?

Therefore the book remains sealed and the plan is not implemented to completion; there is no kingdom of peace and righteousness arising from anything fallen world powers can produce. And so John weeps much (v. 4). The prospect of nothing in the universe or in heaven being able to implement God's plan to satisfy his law and justice for those who are sinners is both tragically alarming to John, and emotionally crushing.

We need to learn a clear lesson here; while many who claim to be Christians see their mission as one of making the world a better place, the reality, and the testimony of scripture, is that this world is broken and beyond repair. God's objective, as we shall see, is not to repair the world but to sweep it away in final judgment and retribution, and replace it with his glorious kingdom. I am not saying that believers should not bother trying to do good in this world where they can, but they should be clear as to the limitations of what they might achieve.

John is distraught at the scene before him; there is the plan of God to save sinners from the just condemnation of their sins, but there is no one found worthy to carry it out to completion. Then in verse 5 one of the twenty-four elders speaks to him telling him there is no need to weep; the case is not lost after all. How does this elder know? Quite simply, he knows because he is in heaven. He represents the church triumphant in glory, enjoying perfect communion with God. Though a sinner when on earth he is now justified and sanctified for he is in the presence of God. He is clothed with the righteousness of God without which no man shall see God. He knows the success of the plan for he sees it outside of time from the perspective of eternity, and he says to John, representing the church militant and still on earth, "Weep not."

The Lion And The Lamb
Why should John "Weep not"? The elder tells John to look at a lion who has prevailed to open the book and loose its seals (v. 5). Though all creation is unable to come up with anyone qualified to implement God's plan, there is a lion in the midst of God's throne, God's seat of universal power. He is the lion of the tribe of Judah (Genesis 49:9, 10). He holds the sceptre of absolute power ruling his people until Shiloh comes, a picture of Christ. He is the 'root of David'. In Isaiah 11:1 we read of a

43

rod coming forth from the stem of Jesse, David's father, and a Branch growing out of his roots, described in Isaiah 4:2 as 'beautiful and glorious'. In Revelation 22:16 we read, 'I Jesus have sent mine angel to testify unto you these things in the churches. I am the root and offspring of David, and the bright and morning star.' Because Christ is the Root of David he came according to the flesh by descent from David.

The elder, representing all saints[5] in heaven, tells John and therefore us here and now, of a King, symbolised by a lion, who has been found worthy to implement God's kingdom plan. Rejoice! Do not weep. Do you believe Christ and his gospel of accomplished, effectual, salvation? Then you have an eternal home in heaven which is certain and sure, reserved for you, that cannot be taken away. As the apostle Peter wrote in 1 Peter 1:3-5, 'Blessed be the God and Father of our Lord Jesus Christ, which according to his abundant mercy hath begotten us again unto a lively hope by the resurrection of Jesus Christ from the dead, To an inheritance incorruptible, and undefiled, and that fadeth not away, reserved in heaven for you, Who are kept by the power of God through faith unto salvation ready to be revealed in the last time.'

In verse 6 something unexpected happens. John looks towards the lion in the midst of God's throne, as he was bidden to do by the elder, but he does not see a lion; he sees a living Lamb that had clearly once been slain. Surely the Lion has overcome and loosed the seals, but how? Only in the capacity of a Lamb, and a Lamb for the slaughter. Where the Lion speaks of kingly strength and power, the Lamb speaks of silent submission. Isaiah 53:7 tells us, 'he is brought as a lamb to the slaughter' bearing the marks of sacrifice and death but clearly alive. And though he is a silently submissive Lamb, yet he has seven horns of divine power, not the ten of world power, and seven eyes indicating the fulness of God's Spirit upon him.

Why does this representation of the Lion make him worthy to loose the seals and implement God's plan? The kingdom of justified sinners made kings and priests unto God (v. 10) can be implemented and established only if satisfaction is first made to God's infinite holiness and justice, which must condemn and punish sin. The Lion, having been slain as a Lamb and as a substitute for his elect people has fully and completely satisfied everything the offended law of God has demanded from those people, i.e. their punishment and death. Hence, he is worthy to loose the

---

[5] In scripture, saints are simply 'set apart ones', Christ's believing people, not especially holy people as the Roman Catholic Church counts holiness.

seals and implement the establishment of God's kingdom. He comes therefore (v. 7), and takes the book.

The Citizens And Their Praise

From verse 8 to the end of the chapter, we see the church's response to seeing the Lamb take the book. Harps indicate prophecy and preaching, prayers indicate devotion and consecration to God. They all fall down in willing, gladsome worship and declare, 'Thou art worthy!'. The Lord Jesus Christ is worthy to implement God's kingdom because he was slain to redeem his people with his own life-blood thereby paying the price, the sin-debt to the law, for them and for us.

Now John sees an innumerable multitude of people from every kindred, tongue and nation. For God so loved the world of his elect people without distinction of race, language or gender, that he gave his only begotten Son to redeem them (John 3:16). They all unite in praise and give all the glory to God ascribing praise and honour to the Lamb.

Are you a citizen of God's kingdom? Is your home the Celestial City or the Vanity Fair of Bunyan's *Pilgrim's Progress*? What qualifies you to apply for citizenship? Simply a God-given thirst for righteousness and a conscious and heavy burden of sin. If you know anything of these things, then Christ says to you, "Come unto me and I will give you rest for your souls."

The Kingdom Of God Triumphant

Chapter 6

Four Seals Opened

Revelation 6:1-8

Look at the world around us; we are provided with a constant stream of news, rarely good, often completely unexpected. At the time of writing an earthquake has just struck central Italy killing at least 250 people. In addition to natural disasters, the world's political scene seems to be in constant turmoil.

How do we explain the way things are? Many seem confused and uncertain except perhaps for today's evolutionary scientists who express unflinching confidence in their materialistic paradigm of big-bang beginnings and development of all life from a primordial soup of basic building blocks. Philosophers say there is far more to it but they, too, fail to provide any satisfactory answers. History is littered with examples of worldly-wise people who claim to know the meaning of life but end up taking their own lives in suicidal despair at life's pointlessness.

There have been many writers and many books claiming to foretell the future, each attempting with some measure of certainty to predict future events; but they all get it dead wrong. How about a book that is almost two thousand years old that is still getting it absolutely right? That is the book of Revelation; we all need to pay careful attention to its message.

Principles Of Interpretation
Let us recap on what we have seen so far. Revelation comprises seven distinct visions, each covering either the whole of created history or the period from Christ's ascension to his second coming at the end of time. Each one has a different perspective on the same reality and, as they progress towards the end, the level of detail regarding the end of all things increases. The visions are not a sequence of physical, historical, events as many falsely claim. Such and similar approaches lead to all sorts of weird views. We must remember the purpose for which The Revelation

is given; it is to assure and comfort God's people regarding the unfolding of history as God establishes his kingdom of righteousness and peace. The kingdom for which Christ taught us to pray, 'Thy Kingdom come'.

Chapters 1 to 3 showed us the church of Christ in this world throughout the time from his ascension to his return. We saw that Christ is actively moving among his people, in his churches; guiding, rebuking, encouraging. We are assured that this space-time world in which we live is limited in duration, that Satan's worldly kingdom will be completely overthrown and God's unrivalled kingdom of righteousness and peace will have the final and eternal victory. But for now, the churches are in a wilderness separation from the world, with the risen, glorified Christ in the midst of them keeping and feeding them.

In chapters 4 through 7 we have the second vision of the whole book; we are given a view of heavenly realities, removed from this world of physical senses but every bit as real. We saw a throne, a majestic king, a blessed people in eternal bliss and all things subject to the rule of God. Then in chapter 5 we saw a book with seven seals and we saw that this is nothing less than the plan for the final accomplishment of God's victorious kingdom. We heard about a call that went out to find anyone qualified to implement the plan. That call went unanswered for which the apostle John wept much. But his grief was turned to rejoicing when an elder pointed out to him the Lion of the Tribe of Judah. John looked and saw a Lamb clearly having been slain. The Lion is the Christ of God, but he is qualified to implement the plan only in the capacity of a slain Lamb. The sinners who will comprise the citizens of God's blessed kingdom must, and can only be justified by the substitutionary sacrifice of the Lamb of God.

Now we have a plan for implementing the eternal purposes of God's kingdom and we have one who is uniquely qualified to implement it, the Lord Jesus Christ. Hence we are now in a position to embark upon the opening of the seals and in chapter 6, the first six of the seven seals are opened. In this chapter let us look at the first four seals.

Why Does God's Kingdom Need To Come?
In Genesis chapters 1 and 2 we have the account of God's creation. In the Garden of Eden we have a picture of God's kingdom in an unrivalled state, God and man communing together. Adam and Eve walked in perfect fellowship with their Creator. There was no sin evident, only righteousness and peace. But God permitted Satan, who had already rebelled, to beguile Eve into disobedience against God and, for love of Eve, Adam too, plunged himself into the same rebellion and all creation

with him. In effect, Adam delivered himself and his kingdom, for God had delegated authority over the created order to Adam, into Satan's dominion and power, and Adam became Satan's ally in opposition to God. Perhaps it was for this reason that Satan told Jesus in his wilderness temptation that the kingdoms of the world were his to give to whomsoever he chose (Matthew 4:8, 9).

Satan's objective, ever since he beguiled Eve, has been to have the victory over God with his kingdom of counterfeit righteousness and false peace. The Fall was Satan's crucial accomplishment. But as soon as the Fall occurred, God immediately struck back at Satan by regenerating Adam and Eve (Genesis 3:15) thereby putting enmity between all who are of Satan and those regenerated by God's Spirit. Right there in Genesis chapter 3 we witness the gospel of gracious salvation from sin and see the battle lines drawn between the good of God and the evil of Satan.

The enmity has continued and does so right to this day. Cain, the seed of Satan, was at enmity with Abel, the seed of the saved woman. We read of the 'sons of God' and the 'daughters of men' mixing by lust and fleshy enticement, Satan's objective being to steal from the 'sons of God' their allegiance to God their Father. This struggle continued and intensified until the flood when God swept all the work of Satan into hell saving only those eight objects of his grace. Noah and his family were shut up in the ark for safety. Yet, no sooner did subsequent human civilisation prosper and grow but Nimrod, the 'mighty rebel', set up Babel and its tower to reach to heaven. This became Babylon, the symbol later in Revelation of all opposition to Christ and his gospel. Here again we see Satan's kingdom established and dominant, and what is it but a kingdom of falsehood that promises the attainment of eternal happiness without the need for satisfaction of divine justice, a kingdom with no Christ and therefore no true righteousness.

God frustrated Satan's purpose at Babel; human language was 'confused' into multiple, mutually incomprehensible languages and thus the nations of the world were established. With nations came wars as men sought riches, power and all that would satisfy their fleshy desires. Then Abraham was called of God and God's 'nation' was established through faith and warfare of a different kind ensued, spiritual warfare. To this day the 'seed of Abraham' (Hebrews 2:16) is in opposition spiritually to all the worldly nations who in various ways try to establish their own world-wide kingdom of godless righteousness and false harmony. Despite man's attempts to remove national barriers, to set up free movement without borders, to enable seamless communication around the world, in the providence of God, all these efforts are constantly frustrated by war, economic strife and death.

None of us relishes war, and the consequential poverty, sickness and death that follows, but true Christians need to be aware that these things are in fact God's instruments to frustrate the objectives of Satan. As Christians we do not seek a utopia in this world, though we ought to do whatever we reasonably can to relieve suffering on a personal level. Our prayer is that God's kingdom should come, not that Satan's kingdom should be improved. This is what we see in Revelation 6:1-8 with its four horses.

The Four Horses
As believers we look at the apparent chaos in the world around us and see the evident godlessness of men and women. Often, there is temptation to imagine that things are out of control. People ask the question, "Where is God in all this?" We see disaster, hear of a war with its poverty and suffering. Well, what does God's seven-sealed book tell us?

As we have seen, this book is God's plan for the implementation of his unrivalled kingdom. The only One found, the only person qualified to implement the plan – pictured by the opening of the book's seals – is the Lion of the Tribe of Judah, the Lord Jesus Christ himself. But notice that the Lord's qualification to open the seals is only in the capacity of a slain Lamb. Nevertheless, it is him, and him alone, our God manifested to us in Christ, who opens the seals and unfolds history; these do not just happen. In spiritual signification, the Lamb calls forth four horses, not quietly but with the noise of thunder. Horses are symbolical of power and nobility in their various missions and each one has a rider to direct the power called forth. Let me be clear about this matter. Things are the way they are, the way we see them unfolding in world history, because the Lamb of God calls forth these four spiritually symbolical horses. There are no accidents with God, no surprises. Let us understand what these horses mean.

The White Horse – the first way that God frustrates the purposes of Satan is by sending his Christ into the kingdoms of this world. In the vision, Christ, the king of God's kingdom, rides majestically with his crown of supreme authority and with his whiteness depicting perfect righteousness. His bow symbolises that he is armed to subdue his enemies. In Old Testament days, national Israel was a frustration to Satan's purposes of godless utopia. In the temple worship, with priests, offerings and sacrifices, propitiation for sin was made and foreshadowed and the satisfaction of offended divine justice was portrayed in symbol.

Then Christ himself came and finished the work of redemption. Ever since then the gospel of grace, declaring justification and conversion of sinners made righteousness by God in Christ, has been proclaimed to the frustration of Satan. This is the unfolding plan for the establishment of God's unrivalled kingdom. Then there is,

The Red Horse – and once again we see the plan unfold for the establishment of God's kingdom. The Lamb calls forth the red horse to disrupt Satan's objectives. The red horse is symbolical of war; it has power to take peace from the earth and set nation against nation. Rather than all nations uniting in a supposed utopian world kingdom we discover continual warring and rumours of wars. There were wars from the moment the languages were confused at Babel but nothing ever came close to the scale of carnage and suffering endured in the first half of the 20th Century. Despite the League of Nations, the United Nations, councils, conferences and many other alliances such as the European Union, wars continue and become ever more difficult to stop. As we have already said, we do not rejoice in war; how could we? We are for peace, yet we nevertheless recognise that war, symbolised by the calling forth of the red horse, is part of God's purpose to frustrate Satan achieving his objective. What else?

The Black Horse – this horse symbolises scarcity and famine. Look at the enormously wide spectrum of human prosperity in the world; the majority seem to live in hand-to-mouth poverty while some wallow in overwhelming abundance. The earth is able to produce food and resources enough for seven billion people but despite that, what we see throughout the world when the black horse is summoned and rides forth is economic strife. And what a stimulus to conflict and war that produces.

The Pale Horse – the colour of this horse is greyish green; it evokes sickness and death. We are told that a quarter of the earth's population is directly affected by it. And is not this our experience? Despite claims for longevity and suggestions that we are all living much longer on average than our forebears, sickness and death continue to mow down great swathes of humanity; indeed, who is immune to it?

From The Fall With One Objective
From the time of the Fall into sin in the Garden of Eden, all of the symbolical four horses have gone forth under the Lamb's direction and done so with the clear objective of frustrating Satan's kingdom in its purpose and dominion. Thereby, God's kingdom of righteousness and peace is protected, preserved and ultimately will be victorious. Yet, all

51

four horses and their horsemen affect all kinds of people. All mankind without distinction are subject to the works of God that are symbolised by the horses and none are immune from their influence, not even God's elect in the world.

Just as the white horse of the gospel calls God's elect out of Satan's kingdom of darkness, it also affects many in Satan's kingdom. This is evident not only in the abundance of false Christianity we see in the world today, but also in the way the gospel's influence restrains evil and in inspires genuine good works being done in the name of religion, even though these effects stop short of true, saving faith in those touched by it. Similarly, war, economic strife, sickness and death affect people throughout the world without distinction, including God's true believing people.

Why does the going forth of these horses have such dramatic effect upon the history of this world? The simple and obvious response is that their purpose is to prevent the premature establishment of the imitation-kingdom of Anti-Christ, of which we shall speak more in later chapters. The red, black and pale horses contrive to derail world powers, rendering them far too busy and distracted in their own inadequacies to be able to launch a final attack on the children of God's kingdom.

What are we to conclude from this Revelation of God's purpose? Believer, be comforted and be encouraged. All things are under God's direct control. We know that all things work together for good to them that love God, to them who are the called according to his purpose (Romans 8:28), and 'all things' include wars, political upheaval, economic strife, sickness and even death.

Are there any reading this who have not believed the gospel? Will you not consider that this is by far the most credible explanation for the way things are and have always been in the world? If you agree with that, why will you not believe God about sin, judgment and salvation?

Chapter 7

Rest For A Little Season

Revelation 6:9-17

In recent years the old gospel way-marks have been steadily and purposefully removed by those that once claimed to be 'pillars of the truth' regarding the gospel of Christ. Recently, I read the bulletin of one church that used to stand solidly for the good news of salvation accomplished in the person and work of Christ. What we call the gospel of sovereign grace and particular redemption. The bulletin contained a short article from a para-church organisation stating that the Bible is, essentially, a 'handbook for living'. Now, it is undoubtedly true that the Bible provides excellent direction on right and wrong ways to live, but it is by no means its main purpose. Failure to mention its primary and principle purpose and replacing it with guidelines for living is deceitful, and ultimately damaging to the cause of Christ. The Bible is God's word to his elect telling them how he has justified them in Christ, despite them being his implacable enemies and dead in sin. He also tells them how he keeps them in their worldly sojourn and how his kingdom is being established and shall finally triumph. When the risen Christ opened the understanding of his disciples (Luke 24:45) that they might understand the scriptures, he caused them to know and handle the word this way. They did not to regard it as a set of rules and regulations for positive and successful living but as the revelation of the gospel of God's grace to sinners delivered from just condemnation.

This is entirely consistent with the opening by Christ of the seven-sealed book seen here in Revelation; that book is God's plan for the establishment of his unrivalled kingdom of true peace and righteousness. His plan for saving his elect and bringing them to eternal glory. The question posed in Revelation 5:2 asked who was worthy to implement this plan of salvation. There was utter silence. Nothing in the world and nothing in the domain of Satan responded, for nothing in this world and nothing in Satan's kingdom could satisfy divine justice or accomplish the salvation of God's elect sinners. We must never look to these failed pretenders as many in so-called Christian religion do. This is merely clutching at straws. There is only one way that God's salvation is accomplished and that is by God's Son who said of himself, "I am the way, the truth and the life". He is the Lion of the Tribe of Judah to whom John was directed to look and he alone is able to save his people in the capacity of the Lamb that was slain. His death, his shed blood, and his alone, has satisfied divine justice for his elect.

We who believe the gospel are left here in this world until either we die or Christ comes to take us out of it. How are we to understand what we see in history, world news, politics, religion, war and the steady march of so-called civilisation? Is it just the random, meaningless product of evolution? The 'fool' of Psalm 14 fools himself with that empty notion; the people of God on the other hand listen to God's voice.

The First Four Seals Opened
We saw in Revelation 6:1-8 the opening by Christ of the first four seals of the seven-sealed book. In summary, the story of the last 2000 years since John wrote Revelation has been first, the White Horse of the gospel of Christ touching swathes of humanity, some with regenerating truth and faith, others with reprobate religion and a false kingdom of imitation peace and righteousness. Second, the Red Horse bringing individual enmity and wars between nations. Third, economic strife which seems never to improve despite the best of intentions by some to make poverty history. And, fourth, death and sickness afflicting mankind in every age. That this is an accurate summary of the history of the last two millennia is indisputable, but Revelation has told us not only the what, but the why. All four of these horses have been sent forth by God into this world, which is the kingdom of Satan. Their united purpose is to frustrate Satan's desire to establish a worldwide kingdom of false peace and sham-righteousness without securing satisfaction of divine justice. Aspirations of a worldly utopia have been constantly thwarted by God who has at the same time implemented his plan of effectual salvation by the death of Christ. With this understanding, we now proceed to look at the opening of the fifth and sixth seals of the book.

The Fifth Seal Opened
Please read verses 9 to 11. Remember this book is largely symbolical with a few passages clearly intended to be taken literally. It is generally quite straightforward to discern the passages that are literal but these verses are full of symbolism and that is how we must interpret them.

The opening of this fifth seal pictures the church of Christ in opposition to the kingdom of this world, opposition that reaches its peak in the martyrdom of God's gospel-believing people. The kingdom of Satan hates the word of God and the testimony of its truth to the extent that it is willing to destroy it and slay its messengers if it can. It makes martyrs of faithful witnesses, killing them in order to silence them. In verse 10 they, the martyrs, cry out for vengeance, not out of hatred or vindictiveness but on account of violated justice. Just as Abel's blood cries out from the ground for justice (Hebrews 12:24) so does the blood of the martyrs shed for their faith.

But it does not speak only of those literally martyred for their faith; it speaks of all of God's elect in this world, living in opposition to the principles and values of this world. You see, these souls are 'under the altar'. They are in the place where the blood of the atoning sacrifice poured down (see Leviticus 4:7) symbolising the place of redemption in Christ's blood (Colossians 1:14; Hebrews 9:12). Indeed, though animal sacrifices in the temple in Jerusalem ended in AD 70 as Daniel prophesied they would, Hebrews 13:10 assures believers that 'we have an altar'. That altar is Christ and the redemption he has accomplished in his death and by his blood. Eternal bliss and peace with God is only for those who have the righteousness of God and that is only accomplished by Christ's redeeming blood making satisfaction to the violated law of God. It is experienced only by Holy Spirit regeneration and once you have it you can never lose it. But, similarly, once you have it you cannot deny it and the world, Satan's kingdom, will hate you for it. Thousands have been butchered, and in some places still are, because of the hatred of the kingdoms of this world, political and religious, against Christ (Matthew 24:9). What is at the root of this hatred? The kingdoms of this world despise the notion that their own perceived goodness is not the required righteousness of God; they will not confess their sin before God and they will silence God's people who insist upon it. They refuse to hear they are under the just condemnation of God, who alone is holy. They hate that they are impotent to change that fact. But above all they are repulsed by the idea that God should save his elect according to nothing other than his sovereign grace and particular redemption. This is the essence of man's sin and rebellion against God.

Now, while thousands of believers have been martyred for their faith many more have been, and continue to be, afflicted by the opposition of this world and its systems, including all that calls itself 'Christian' but in reality is nothing but the 'synagogue of Satan' (Revelation 3:9). We are instructed by God's word to try to live at peace with all men (Romans 12:18), but when we speak of the word of God and the testimony we hold, the response is often hatred and a desire to silence the witness. Some who hear might be brought to believe but there is a black and white separation. To some our message is a savour of death unto death but to others, by God's grace, it is a savour of life unto life (2 Corinthians 2:14).

Thus, the fifth seal is the experience God has ordained for his people living in this worldly kingdom of Satan, all of it, do not forget, for their eternal good (Romans 8:28). Whenever true Christians stand firm for the truth of God and the testimony of redemption from the law's curse by Christ, the political and religious world hates them. They talk of religious freedom but it seems like freedom for all except those who faithfully seek to maintain gospel truth. In these days in 'civilised' western cultures, the world's persecution of the gospel may be mild opposition such as being ignored or ostracised. It is increasingly persecution upon the footing of 'politically correct' values. Nevertheless, the effects can be personally devastating for example, when individuals are compelled to act against their principles or lose their jobs, and small companies are threatened with closure for not adopting current mores. It is difficult to be a Christian science teacher because any belief in 'intelligent design' in the natural world is dogmatically and unscientifically opposed by the mainstream scientific community whose influence strongly and understandably guides schools in the appointment of science teachers. One can easily envisage this situation escalating to a place where it is difficult for some Christians to earn a living in an otherwise increasingly liberal society. The text of Revelation 6 indicates at the end of verse 11 that there will be more actual martyrdom of true believers before the end. We should not worry, 1 John 3:13 tells us not to be surprised if the world hate us. It hated our Lord.

The Martyrs' Cry Answered
Those martyred cry out asking how long justice must delay (v. 10), how long until the vengeance of God brings just punishment and retribution on those who persecuted and martyred believers. The answer is given in verse 11. First, the martyrs who cry are given white robes; every one of them without exception. I see no degrees of reward in heaven. God is the exceeding great reward of all his people (Genesis 15:1). All God's saints, all his 'set-apart ones', who are saints by virtue of nothing other than their belief of the truth of the gospel, all those either literally martyred or the many more who for Christ's sake are 'killed all the day long' (Romans 8:36), are assured of their 'acceptance in the Beloved', all of

them made to be the righteousness of God in Christ who was made sin for them in order to pay its debt. If you are believing in Christ, resting in the gospel of his grace, whatever worldly hatred or even martyrdom might be in store, you are assured of justification before the law of God, and you are promised a white robe.

But when will this be? Look at verse 11. It will be when all God's people, the hated and martyred in all ages, are 'fulfilled'. It will be when all the elect of God, all those 'ordained to eternal life' (Acts13:48) have believed the gospel in accordance with the work of the White Horse, the first seal, to frustrate Satan's intentions. In other words, it is all in God's providential, sovereign control and there is nothing for believers to fear. But, to further underline the fact that this world will not continue indefinitely, the sixth seal is now opened.

The Sixth Seal Opened
Please read verses 12 to 17. I believe this is a part of God's answer to the prayers of his church for just retribution on the kingdoms of the world. The sixth seal appears to be a preparation of this physical creation for Christ's return, for the final judgment, the final overthrow of Satan's kingdom and the triumph of God's kingdom.

The signs of the sixth seal involve physical and astronomical phenomena. I am aware some insist on interpreting these words in purely spiritual terms but it seems to me to be stretching language in a way that is not called for here. As noted earlier, throughout Revelation it is fairly clear where the language is symbolic and where it is literal and we can therefore discern its spiritual significance accordingly. All we need be aware of, and beware of, is attempting to mix literal and symbolical interpretations in the same passage as it usually leads to confusion. Here, I believe the emphasis is on literal interpretation. The signs of the end of this created order are marked by real, physical phenomena; earthquakes, the sun being darkened, the moon's light altered and meteor showers.

Cosmologists tell us that it will be five billion years before the sun engulfs the earth as a red giant; God's word warns us always to regard the end as imminent. The end, according to this sixth seal, will be marked by geological and astronomical cataclysms; it is coming and the seal is already opened by the one who alone is qualified. When it comes to its climax all those great worldly persecutors of God's people will be in a state of utter terror, pleading for their own annihilation. Sceptics might retort that to hold such a view indicates madness, as they did with Paul (Acts 26:24). But throughout history God has testified to the certainty of

57

this end of all things. The world-wide flood of Noah's day, the destruction of Sodom and Gomorrah, earthquakes, tsunamis, meteor impacts and an increasing awareness of astronomical 'near-misses', all give notice that 'the end' of which God's word speaks so clearly, is both certain and imminent. The key question to ask is whether you are ready for that end when it comes. It is something to which Christ often pointed in his earthly ministry, for example, in Luke 17:20-37. Are you in a state of prepared and ready anticipation?

Chapter 8

Sealed For Tribulation, Certain Of Glory

Revelation 7

In my thirties I learned the true gospel through listening to cassette tapes of the preaching of Henry Mahan, Don Fortner and others[6]. I could not get enough of it. It was, and still is, better than any teaching at a theological seminary! In one message, Henry Mahan gave an illustration that has stuck with me regarding the end of all things; he said that he loved watching basketball games on TV, especially those involving his beloved University of Kentucky team, but he could not stand the stress of watching live. He would wait for the game to be over and if it was a good result, only then he would watch a recording. Now, I realise this approach is at odds with the preferred way of most sports fans who love the excitement of the live match, even if the result goes against their team. But when it comes to the unfolding of world history and the end of all things I am so glad that the Holy Spirit has revealed the final outcome to his people beforehand. He allows us to observe the progression of world events in the certain knowledge of the final outcome so we need not be anxious about any of it. The purpose of Revelation was given in Revelation 1:1; it is to show, signified by an angel to John, 'unto his servants things which must shortly come to pass'.

This world is Satan's kingdom of imitation, false, fraudulent good. Even what seems innocuous will turn out to be a lie because Satan is the 'father of lies'. But God's word assures his people that Satan's kingdom will certainly be defeated and destroyed as Christ's kingdom is established in absolute, eternal supremacy. Christ the King is coming to defeat Satan's kingdom and reign supreme. However, many alarming things must yet happen along the way, things affecting all humanity. Revelation 6:17 asks 'who shall be able to stand'? Revelation chapter 7 provides the answer.

---

[6] Many of these messages and more can be found today on the internet at www.freegraceradio.com, a 'filter' for www.sermonaudio.com preachers who specifically focus on preaching free, sovereign, grace.

A Reminder Of The Six Opened Seals

We have seen that the seven-sealed book (Revelation 5:1) represents God's plan for the establishment of his unrivalled kingdom. The only one found worthy to implement the plan, to open its seals, is the Lion of the Tribe of Judah and he only in the capacity of a slain Lamb. The Lamb must be slain to justify the citizens of God's kingdom by answering the demands of God's offended justice. But enmity continues as Satan constantly tries to establish his unrivalled kingdom of fake peace and phoney righteousness. Throughout history Satan has endeavoured to set up his world kingdom in opposition to God. We have seen a repeating pattern from the Fall in Eden. First there was the attempt to dilute the 'sons of God' with the 'daughters of men', culminating in the flood when God swept all away save Noah and his family. Then, at Babel, the united peoples of earth, descendants of Noah, sought to reach heaven without satisfying divine justice. God confounded their efforts. Later, the great empires of the ancient world by conquering and assimilating all the nations before them sought to fulfil Satan's aim of uniting the peoples of the world in opposition to the just demands of God. And it has continued the same right up to today's modern, tolerant, liberal democracies. The enmity continues. Satan uses physical weapons, he uses the will of sinful man, he uses philosophy, materialism, ideology to work his works. Yet he has not succeeded.

Christ's kingdom is not of this world (John 18:36) so no physical weapons are used by his servants, rather spiritual ones (2 Corinthians 10:4, 5). But Christ does send out four symbolical horses into Satan's kingdom to frustrate his designs. He sends the gospel, he sends wars, socio-economic strife and death. It is necessary to keep in mind that God's purpose is not to make Satan's kingdom better but to destroy it and establish his own unrivalled kingdom. God is not, as some seem to portray him, wringing his hands in sorrowful frustration at the wars, disasters, poverty and death throughout Satan's kingdom. He is the one who dispatches the horses that bring about those things. Many professing Christians seem more engaged in attempting to improve Satan's kingdom than in preaching the gospel of grace and salvation. Whilst individually and locally, the Lord's people should seek to do good to all, the true church's message is not, 'Let's Make Poverty History', it is 'Believe On The Lord Jesus Christ And Thou Shalt Be Saved'.

The fifth seal opened revealed the ongoing state of enmity between the kingdoms of Satan and Christ with the blood of the martyrs crying out for justice, and the sixth seal revealed the created universe increasingly showing signs of the end and impending judgment. The message is clear, things will become worse and worse in the run up to the end of this created order. We will see greater levels of detail revealed in later chapters but for now, lest God's people become unduly alarmed at what is revealed, Revelation chapter 7 provides a reassuring answer to the question posed at the end of Revelation 6, namely, 'who shall be able to stand?'.

The Sealing Of The 144,000

The sixth seal at the end of Revelation 6 speaks of a certain end and judgment of all things; it also seems there will be great awareness of its coming but no repentance amongst the generality of mankind and their leaders (v. 15). So as we move into chapter 7 of Revelation we would expect the seventh seal to be opened but, notably, that does not happen. Instead, Revelation 7 stands as an interlude before the seventh seal unfolds as seven trumpets sounding at the start of chapter 8. As the trumpets are sounded increasing detail is given until the seventh trumpet unfolds in the pouring out of seven vials of wrath. In fact, Revelation 7 reassures God's saints of the end result lest they become overwhelmed with the alarming pictures of the gradual and final overthrow of Satan's kingdom. It is a bit like Henry Mahan knowing the final score before he sits down to watch the ebb and flow of the match.

The picture at the start of Revelation 7 is one of judgment ready to fall on creation. Four is the Biblical number of the physical creation. The four angels of judgment stand ready to let loose that judgment on the created order of earth, sea and trees or vegetation, but they are 'holding' back the four winds of judgment that they should not yet blow. Then, in verse 2, John sees another angel who is evidently Christ, the 'righteous man from the east' (Isaiah 41:2) who has the seal, the authority, of the living God. He it is who commands the angels of judgment to hold back until the servants of God have been sealed in their foreheads. This signifies that all God's elect must be called out of their darkness into his marvellous light before the final judgment is set loose.

The seal in the forehead speaks of a clear mark of ownership; it is in a prominent and obvious place. When my oldest son was under a year old I was playing with him and making him laugh by sticking a toy with a rubber-sucker foot on my forehead. The problem was that it became rather firmly attached and when my wife managed to remove it many blood vessels in my forehead had burst leaving a dark purple ring that lasted for several days. This caused great amusement among brethren at the church we attended at the time as it reminded them either of this mark of sealing, or the mark of the Beast of Revelation 14. Of course, a literal, visible ring of burst blood vessels is not what the sealing of Revelation 7 means. So what does it signify? Well, 2 Corinthians 1:21, 22 speaks of God who has 'sealed us' and given us the earnest of the Spirit. Ephesians 1:13 talks of conversion to Christ and the sealing with that Holy Spirit of promise that accompanies belief of the gospel. Ephesians 4:30 exhorts believers not to grieve the Holy Spirit of God whereby they are sealed unto the day of redemption. This sealing is conversion. It is God's Holy Spirit quickening the objects of the Father's grace, when they are dead in trespasses and sins; children of wrath even as others (Ephesians 2:1-4). It is the granting of repentance, the gift of faith, assurance of justification and sanctification. It is stamping upon them his indelible seal of permanent ownership. Before final judgment is permitted by God to fall upon this created order, all of his elect must be brought to Christ in faith.

Every single one of God's elect, every one for whom Christ died, must be brought to a living faith in the Son of God. He purchased their redemption from the law's condemnation, every last one of them. And every one of them must be sealed with God's stamp of ownership. Therefore, whatever happens during this fearful time of judgment to trouble or physically affect any of God's saints alive on earth, they are all without exception completely spiritually immune from any harm. This is the confident message of John 10:27-30, 'They shall never perish'. Child of God, be comforted with this assurance from God's word: whatever comes to pass in terms of judgment on this created order, you will be kept safe and taken to eternal glory at the end.

But why do we read of 144,000? There are many weird and diverse interpretations. Jehovah's Witnesses, for example, say there are precisely 144,000 super JWs who are already in heaven. Others imagine 144,000 Jews will be saved by national privilege. But Romans 9-11; Galatians 3 and 4; and especially Galatians 6:16; all make clear that God's true Israel is his elect people comprising Jew and Gentile without any national barriers. True Israel are the people who have Abraham's spiritual faith irrespective of whether they have his physical genes.

It seems to me this number, 144,000, is a symbolical number rather than anything to be taken literally. In verses 5 to 8 the number is broken down by tribe but, although very close to the names of Jacob's sons, these names do not conform exactly to the names of the 12 tribes. Manasses (Manasseh) was a 'half tribe' and we do not actually read of a tribe of Joseph except in respect of him being father of Manasseh. So it is reasonable to take 144,000 as a symbolical number and I believe that it represents the sealed, converted sinners in the world at any period of time, those sealed against the tribulation of judgment. Do you remember the 7,000 of Elijah's time, when the prophet despaired that only he was left a prophet of the Lord? The Lord reassured him he had his 7,000 who had not bowed the knee to Baal. Seven is God's number of perfection, 1000 is 10 cubed, like the Holy of Holies in the temple, and 10 is the number of completeness, so 7,000 is God's perfect, complete number. However small the visible church seems to be at any point in time, we may be assured there are, in fact, exactly the number that God has called to newness of life in his Son.

Let us think some more about these numbers. We read of 12 tribes and 12 apostles; 12+12=24, the precise number of the elders pictured in heaven around the throne of God (Revelation 4:4). But note also that 12x12=144. Likewise, 3 is the number of God and 4 the number of creation, so 3+4=7 speaks of the perfect union of the church with its head, but also, 3x4=12 speaks of the grace of God exerted on his people in the world. Multiply this again by the 10x10x10 symbolism of the Holy of Holies (compare with Revelation 21:10-17) and you can see, perhaps, something of the symbolical mystery in the number 144,000.

I am, generally speaking, of simple mind. I do not want to attempt to go beyond anything that God has revealed or probe too deeply what he has kept hidden, yet my simple understanding guided by God's Spirit leads me to regard 144,000 as those sealed ones on the earth at any one period of history. They are God's believing people, trusting in Christ for salvation, quickened and sealed by the Holy Spirit. They are those described in Acts 13:48, 'as many as were ordained to eternal life believed'. They are sealed for eternity in preparation for the tribulation to be loosed by the opening of the seventh seal.

The Innumerable Multitude

In verse 9 we see a new vision heralded by the words, 'after this'. Previously we saw 144,000 sealed before the seventh seal is unloosed. But now we see a multitude which is innumerable. To Abraham, God promised descendants as innumerable as the stars or as the sand on the seashore. Do not think that any numerical equivalence is being made between the number of God's elect and the number of grains of sand. The simile is used to convey the inability of anyone to count them, not to try to enforce an utterly implausible equivalence. The simile is just as true today. As much as we are able to look deeper into the universe the more

63

we are convinced we can never count the number of stars, and surely the same applies to the grains of sand on the beaches of the world.

What we see in this new vision is an innumerable multitude of saved people in heaven, people without any distinction of race or language. Jesus told Nicodemus, 'God so loved the world', not just Jews but a world of sinners without distinction of race given to his only begotten Son to save them (John 3:16). These are the sum total of all the 144,000s of every period of history, each one quickened by the Holy Spirit's regenerating power. Each one made willing to trust Christ and receive cleansing from sin in his blood. They have palms in their hands alluding to the Feast of Tabernacles that commemorated the Israelites being led out of the wilderness and into the Land of Promise. The innumerable multitude of the vision have come through their wilderness wanderings of earthly life, of sin and imperfection. They are now in the bliss of heaven, in the eternal 'tabernacle'. They are clothed in white robes (v. 9) having come through great tribulation (v. 14). They are in intimate communion with God and every need is eternally provided for (vv. 15-17).

Their Song
Verses 10 to 12 show us the song of the innumerable multitude. The song is one of praise to God for salvation accomplished. What a glorious accomplishment! Psalm 118:23 poetically summarises it as, 'marvellous in our eyes'. It truly is marvellous. This is an innumerable multitude of sinners deserving, in their natural condition as children of Adam, God's condemnation. They owed an infinite debt to God's broken law and offended justice, yet they are clothed in white in heaven. God has not turned a blind eye to their sin, he has paid their debt to the law in full, in the person of his Son, the Lord Jesus Christ. Thus he is a 'Just God and a Saviour', he is 'just and the justifier of him that believeth in Jesus' (Isaiah 45:21; Romans 3:26). This is the eternal theme of praise to the God of grace.

Conclusion
The opening of the seventh seal will initiate seven trumpets of judgment and the seventh trumpet will release seven vials of divine wrath. The judgment of God has always rested on this world since the Fall but it is going to get worse before the end of all things. It will affect all peoples and God's servants themselves will be affected by it, but they are sealed for heaven and nothing can alter that.

Believer, be comforted by this. This is why God has given us Revelation, to comfort us and save us from alarm. But if you do not believe the Son of God understand you are in peril. Heed the words of John the Baptist to the Pharisees and 'flee from the wrath to come'. Flee to Christ for he has said he will in no wise send away any who come to him burdened with sin (Matthew 11:28; John 6:37).

Chapter 9

Prayer And The Coming Kingdom Of God

Revelation 8

Revelation 8 begins with the opening of the seventh seal of the seven-sealed book which, we have seen, is God's plan for the triumph of his kingdom and the destruction of Satan's. It also marks the beginning of the third vision of the seven visions of the whole book. The second vision from the beginning of Revelation 4 has given us an overview of eternal reality, salvation accomplished, Satan frustrated, and the church finally in glory. Now the seventh seal opens and the third vision reveals seven angels each with a trumpet of judgment to sound. This third vision which occupies chapters 8 to 11, covers the same span of history as the second vision but it provides more detail of certain aspects; it views the same span of world history but from a different perspective. This idea of greater detail from different perspectives is typical of all the remaining visions to follow.

Quickly, let us remind ourselves of the second vision; Revelation 4 showed us God reigning supreme over everything that happens and we must strive to not lose sight of that comforting fact. Then Revelation 5 showed us a seven-sealed book and the only one qualified to implement its plan. Chapter 6 saw the opening of the first six of the seals, these being, first, the white horse of Christ's victorious kingdom, second, the red horse of international discord and war, third, the black horse of socio-economic disharmony and fourth, the pale horse of sickness and death. The fifth seal envisioned perpetual animosity between the kingdom of Satan and the church with God's people crying out for justice, and the sixth seal pointed to increasing portents in the created order of universal cataclysm, culminating in the end of this created order.

All the seals overlap, and though they follow one upon another they may be viewed as successive layers which intensify in their effects towards the end. Then in chapter 7, before the seventh seal is opened, we are assured that final judgment is restrained until all of God's elect people are sealed and marked as belonging to God. This mark of ownership speaks both to themselves directly, they belong to the Lord, but also to anyone else who might enquire of them. These 'sealed ones' are pictured as 144,000 representing God's believing people in the world at any one time in history. Finally, the vision ends with an innumerable multitude, the church triumphant, in the glory of heavenly bliss. Believer, if you struggle to understand, to retain a clear grasp of all that God has revealed, remember the blessing rests not on those who understand but on those who believe these things, or as Revelation 1:3 says, those who read, hear and keep, or lay to heart these truths of God. Let us keep in mind the view we are repeatedly given of the final triumph of God's kingdom and his believing people as citizens of his kingdom.

Silence In Heaven
Does the sovereignty of God ever make you question the purpose of prayer? If everything is ordained of God, why is there a need for prayer? If God's plans are fixed and he is unchangeable, why are we bidden to pray to him? Revelation 8 shows us the place of true, spiritual prayer in the coming of God's kingdom. The world in which believers must live on this earth is, in truth, the kingdom of Satan and everything about it opposes Christ and his salvation. However, it is under sentence of judgment from God, and this judgment is revealed and manifested bit by bit as it intensifies to the final coming of Christ.

For the plan of triumph to be completed the seventh seal must be opened and it is opened when we get to Revelation 8:1. Remember this is a spiritual vision using symbolical language. There is 'silence in heaven about the space of half an hour'; what could this signify? It is not to be taken literally, but it is indicative of a meaningful interval of time. Think about it in our own experience here and now; half an hour is the typical length of a TV or radio programme. It is long enough to get something accomplished but not too long. Seven angels are about to blow seven trumpets of divine judgment, but before they do there is silence for half an hour. Judgment will fall but here we have a brief stay of judgment. It is as though God says, "now, rend your heart and not your garments, and turn unto the Lord your God: for he is gracious and merciful, slow to anger, and of great kindness" (Joel 2:13). Will you heed his voice?

But there is another reason for the half hour of silence. It is for the prayers of all the saints (v. 3). The prayers of those on earth and those in heaven are to be offered, mixed with much incense, to ascend to God. This silence is reverence for the time of prayer. While judgments prepare to fall and increase to the final climax of all things, there is always space, silence in heaven, for the prayers of God's saints to reach his throne. The saints spoken of here, as throughout all scripture, are God's 'sanctified ones', set apart in electing grace in Christ. These are the elect to whom the epistles are addressed, the 144,000 in every period of history, the innumerable multitude in final glory, all of them (v. 3).

All God's people pray. God's Spirit puts it into believers' hearts to pray (2 Samuel 7:27). Praying was the evidence of new spiritual life in Saul of Tarsus to which the Holy Spirit pointed in convincing Ananias to go and minister to the blinded persecutor. But a lot of what even true believers pray is not the prayers spoken of here. Much that we often think of as prayer is tainted by the lusts of the flesh. It is good to 'enquire of the Lord' concerning decisions we need to make in life. Yet I fear too often our prayers concern trivial matters of material well-being; which car to buy, our child's education or career, prayers for health, wealth, safety, and sunny weather, prayers for every traffic light on our journey to go green. Do such prayers ascend mingled with much incense? Rather, the emphasis, because it is emphasis I am talking about, is on the prayers of the saints being prayers from blood-bought, redeemed, justified, sanctified sinners with a focus on the kingdom of God and its triumph. There is a hint here of prayers that need the Spirit's intercession because language fails earth-bound saints (Romans 8:26, 27). Think of what is called, 'the Lord's prayer' in Matthew 6:9-13. Yes, we are encouraged to ask for daily bread, but is not the emphasis upon God's glory, vindication of God and the coming of his triumphant kingdom as seen in the final prayer of Revelation 22:20? Even so come Lord Jesus.

In verse 3 the angel is not one of the seven announced in verse 2. This angel is Christ and it is the incense of his atoning blood that seasons the prayers of all the saints. He, the God-man Christ Jesus, is the one mediator between God and men (1 Timothy 2:5). It is through him alone that the prayers of God's saints for the coming of God's kingdom and the glory of his name are answered. Verse 5 reminds us that judgment is in store for all things here and now. How attached we are, as believers, to the here and now. Yes, by all means, pray we might receive our daily bread, but look up, look to the coming of Christ's kingdom and the overthrow of the god of this world. When you next say, "that was an answer to prayer", question whether you really mean, "I got what I wanted." If Israel, in bondage in Egypt, had identified and aligned itself with Christ-less Egypt, would the people's cry for deliverance have been answered (Exodus 3:9)? If they had identified with Egypt they would have prayed for the plagues to cease!

69

As a general aside, whilst we are thinking along these lines, do we view natural disasters, the atrocities of wicked men and women and other 'news headlines' according to God's word? Individually, as believers, we should strive to help those in need and do to others as we would want them to do to us when in difficulty. But we need always to bear in mind the things that happen in this world, as time rolls towards the end, from natural disasters to the rise and fall of princes, are God's instruments of judgment in the coming of his kingdom.

The First Four Trumpets
Remember seven signifies the union between God symbolised by the number three and his people in the world symbolised by the number four. The effect of God's grace acting on his elect 'children of wrath even as others' (Ephesians 2:4) yet 'ordained to eternal life' (Acts13:48) is at any one time 3x4=12, so we have 12 tribes of Israel, 12 apostles and elders on earth. In the same way, the seven trumpets are like the seven seals in this respect, they are the instruments by which God is bringing about his kingdom. For now we will look at just the first four of the trumpets.

There are many different interpretations of these four trumpets. Men I respect greatly as God's true ministers do not agree with each other on the details so I do not claim to have a definitive interpretation to give you. Yet, this is not a hugely complex jigsaw puzzle into which we must fit every piece until we have a perfect and unique picture. Some whom I respect interpret the trumpets as great forces of natural destruction unleashed upon the earth, for example, on its vegetation resulting in failing crops. Or devastation upon the sea and its seemingly limitless store of food and its usefulness for world-wide transport. Or upon the rivers, suggesting the poisoning of our supplies of fresh water. Or alterations to the astronomical bodies such as sunshine being impeded with devastating effects upon things we take for granted. Others interpret them spiritually as apostasy and error becoming increasingly rampant towards the end. I can accept aspects of both and you will have to make up your own mind. But whatever else they may be the trumpets are certainly the answer of God to the prayers of the saints for Christ's kingdom to come.

The coming of God's triumphant kingdom will see the progressive downfall of Satan's kingdom. The last 200 years have witnessed an explosion in world population; in 1800 world population was estimated to be about one billion people, in 1927 it was 2 billion, in 1960 it was 3 billion, in 1974 it was 4 billion, in 1987 it was 5 billion, in 1999 it was 6 billion and now it is approaching 8 billion. In my lifetime world population has roughly trebled. In parallel with this astonishing fact, and no doubt related to it, scientific knowledge and technology has utterly transformed everyday life for the majority of the world's people. Yet the world, as an environment for supporting life appears to be under increasing threat. We hear about it constantly from the 'green lobby' with its godless, left-wing, agenda. The threats are seen as coming from climate change affecting food production, pollution poisoning natural resources, rapidly spreading incurable diseases, antibiotic resistant bacteria and in addition to all those natural phenomena, the rising threat of terrorism. Furthermore, as if that was not enough, the indebtedness of many of the world's major economies is at an historically unprecedented level with little possibility in view of ever restoring a healthy balance. The first four trumpets could have sounded extremely fanciful when John wrote Revelation over 1900 years ago. Today they seem like typical headline world news.

Is the message not clear that the signs of the end approaching are becoming more tangible? When the seals were opened (Revelation 6:8) the proportion of humanity that death would kill was a quarter; as the trumpets blow the proportion has increased to a third. We have not attempted to be detailed in aligning world events with the details of the trumpets in verses 7 to 12, but there is a clear message. It is in the purpose of God to make this world less able to support comfortable, prosperous, healthy life as the end of time approaches.

Believer, if you are a true believer, Christ's kingdom is your goal and the centre of your desire. Your heart is set on things above where Christ is seated. You know this world is just for a brief while, only until all God's elect have been brought into the blessings of salvation and their prayers for God's kingdom to come have ascended up before God to be answered as they surely will be. Hiding in the shadow of that great Rock Christ (Isaiah 32:2) there is nothing in Revelation 8 to be afraid of. But unbeliever, be wise, look at the signs, heed the warnings of God's word, flee to Christ from the wrath to come. He will not turn you away.

Chapter 10

The First Two Woes

Revelation 9

In Revelation 8 we saw the opening of the third vision of Revelation; the seventh seal had been opened and it issued forth in seven angels each with a trumpet of judgment to sound. The angels are God's ministering spirits (Hebrews 1:14). The judgments they release are at his instigation and command. Keep this clearly in mind.

In this world in which we live, in the 21st century, the pervading view is that man is constantly improving. We are richer, we have smart technology, we are tending to live longer and to overcome disease. And we are more tolerant of diversity[7]. National borders are more open than ever and mass, world-wide travel and high speed communications mark this age out as truly unique in history. We ought not to be hypocritical, most believers enjoy and in many ways benefit greatly from these developments. But simultaneously, believers sense we are living in 'perilous times' (2 Timothy 3:1-5). God's word confirms this to be the case. As fast as a new layer is put on Babel's tower, reaching up to Satan's false heaven, something happens to knock it back down. This is God's doing. We saw some of it in the blast from the first four trumpets whose effects were to damage the ability of the earth to support the ballooning population.

Religious folk ask, "Where is God when disaster strikes?" They struggle to understand the role of God in relation to the 20th Century's world wars, the Holocaust, the 9/11 attack in New York, the 2004 Indian Ocean tsunami, earthquakes, devastating terrorist attacks, persistent poverty and famine, mountainous levels of debt and general moral degeneration. They view God wringing his hands and weeping in frustrated impotence. Revelation, and the passage before us, show true

---

[7] Though most believers would view as perversity much of what the world calls diversity.

believers how to think properly about these matters. Though judgments at first sight are alarming, there is no need to fear. God is in control of everything. The disciples were terrified when they saw a ghostly figure walking on the waves towards their storm-tossed boat, but how their fear turned to peace when they knew it was Christ who then spoke to them comfortably, 'Be of good cheer: it is I; be not afraid' (Mark 6:50).

Three Woes

Remember what we have seen so far concerning the seven-sealed book and the first four trumpets. They all speak of God disrupting Satan's attempts to establish his earthly kingdom of false, Christless peace and counterfeit righteousness. Chapter 7 assured us that whatever we might have to witness and even experience in this world as the judgments proceed and take hold, our eternal safety and destiny as believers is in no doubt. Then, after the first four trumpets have sounded in Revelation 8, the last verse of the chapter warns that three worse judgments are yet to come: three woes.

The seals and the trumpets are contemporaneous throughout world history, especially since Christ's ascension to glory, though there is a clear indication of intensification of them towards the end. For example, where the seals affected a quarter of mankind, the trumpets affect a third. Now, what we see today has always, to some extent, been happening, but with the increase of world population in the last 200 years, together with improved communication, we see the judgments on an unprecedented world-wide scale, affecting many more people. But we need not be alarmed because all these judgments are released by God for the purpose of answering his saints' prayers; for God's kingdom to come and overthrow Satan's kingdom. Indeed, reading of these things, there really is only one genuine cause for alarm and that is if you are outside of Christ.

The First Woe

Please read the first 11 verses of Revelation 9. Understand this is not a sequence in time. It is revealed in eternity, outside of time. The fifth trumpet, the first of the woes, relates to the fall of Satan and hordes of demons with him. Our Lord Jesus spoke of this in Luke 10:18 when he said, "I beheld Satan as lightning fall from heaven."

The scene pictured is of this fallen 'star' who is given a key to let loose a world-wide plague of locusts. This fallen star is Satan, alias Abaddon, alias Apollyon (v. 11). But be sure not to miss the fact that ultimate power is in the hand of the one who gave him the key, surely God. With God's permission, Satan releases spirits, that were bound in the bottomless pit, in the form of locusts with the power of scorpions. It appears these are different from the demonic spirits that do Satan's will 'in the air' (Ephesians 2:2). Could these spirits in the air be the ones against which believers are told we wrestle (Ephesians 6:12) and for which the armour of God is prescribed (Ephesians 6:13-18)?

The demonic spirits released in Revelation 9:2, 3 are prevented from harming Christ's people. They are sent to torment only people who do not have the conversion seal of God in their foreheads (Revelation 7:3). They move like a plague of locusts, terrifying in their ability to wreak destruction on vegetation, but these are forbidden from touching anything beyond the citizens of Satan's kingdom. This is clearly symbolical language for they are locusts shaped like war horses, yet with the alluring appearance of men and women. The image speaks of power, riches, charm and beauty. Sinners outside of Christ willingly choose Satan's works and kingdom. In his indictment of the sinful state of man in Romans 1, Paul describes the withdrawal of God's restraining hand in verse 24 as 'giving them up to uncleanness through the lusts of their own hearts' and what they lust after is exactly what Satan uses to entice them away from gospel truth.

But, just as these locusts are alluring, so, too, they carry a painful sting in their tail (v. 10) like the sting of a scorpion renowned for its painfulness, even deadliness. In verse 6 we see people first allured, then stung and seeking to die to escape the pain, yet not being able to die. The duration of five months speaks of the summer months when the locusts tend to swarm and this is symbolical of a long but limited time. What does it all mean and how should we interpret it?

Satanic forces are shaping the spirit of the age in which we live. There has always been such an influence but rarely more so than today. Sexual perversion reached a peak in Abraham's day at Sodom and Gomorrah so there is nothing new under the sun in that respect, but it has never been more widely practised than it is today throughout the world. Scarcely a day passes without some further twist of perversity coming to the fore, such as a recent children's television programme encouraging children as young as six to be open to the possibility of changing gender. This fifth trumpet is a woe of spiritual proportions, affecting the way people think, the way societies organise themselves, the morals they promote and those they restrain. These Satanic forces control the minds of political leaders, they influence education, they promote depraved arts and dress up vile sin as charming and attractive. What was held as repugnant even 50 years ago is now heralded as inherently good, the only evil being an intolerant spirit. This is the 'course of this world according to the prince of the power of the air' (Ephesians 2:2). Philosophers speak of the 'ascent of man' to use the words of Jacob Bronowski in his 1960s acclaimed television series, but what do you think paints the more accurate picture of the state of man today? That atheistic and materialistic view, or the teaching of Revelation 9?

The first woe tells us this: the one who seduces mankind with the prospect of a Christless kingdom of false peace is actually directing torment and suicidal despair on those he draws away from Christ.

The Second Woe
The second woe is announced by the trumpet of the sixth angel (v. 13). Please read verses 13-21. The picture is of devastating judgment which kills a symbolical third part of mankind (v. 18). The command initiating the judgment comes from the four horns of the golden altar that is before God. This reminds us of the altar of burnt offering and incense in the temple; the blood of the animal sacrifices was to be smeared on the horns of the altar. That blood pointed to the sacrifice of our Lord Jesus Christ and his blood shed for the sins of his people. The blood on the altar horns, prefiguring Christ's blood, speaks better things than the blood of Abel (Hebrews 12:24) because, whereas Abel's blood cried out for justice, Christ's blood speaks of satisfaction made to the offended justice of God. But the peoples of the world around about us everywhere we look, have metaphorically trampled that precious blood underfoot (Hebrews 10:29). They do this by despising it and treating it as irrelevant to their eternal situation. That rejection by mankind in general of the only way of salvation is what causes the voice of Revelation 9:13 to cry out. To reject salvation is the unforgiveable sin. It necessarily calls forth judgment.

But what is the nature of the judgment that is set loose? Four angels, thus far bound in the river Euphrates are released at a precise time, an hour, a day, a month, a year, and it seems that their being loosed brings forth a huge army of 200 million horsemen. It is clear that this is not literal because of the description of the horses. They have heads of lions and serpents for tails; they breathe fire and smoke and brimstone and by them a third of mankind is killed. This is a vision (v. 17) but what does it represent?

Remember it is the response of God to mankind's general rejection of the gospel. The army of horsemen speaks of overwhelming power; it is unstoppable. It comes rapidly at a definite time and the fire it breathes is representative of war[8], the smoke speaks of the desolation of war and the brimstone or sulphur speaks of the pestilence that follows war. Whether this is speaking of another world war yet to come, I cannot tell. What is clear is that God will utterly frustrate Satan's plans for Christless world unity. He will certainly punish sin, especially the sin of rejecting his Son, and he remains in supreme control of all things.

What could the river Euphrates mean here? That river was pictured in the Old Testament for example in Genesis 15:18, as the eastern border of the physical, earthly, kingdom of God, i.e. Israel. To its east lay the godless kingdoms of Gog and Magog, great swathes of humanity relatively untouched by the influence of the gospel or what we might call 'nominal Christendom'. The removal of that border, symbolised by the loosing of the four angels, is what we have seen in recent years in the explosion of world-wide travel and population migration. Compare this with Revelation 16:12. This has led to the dilution and disappearance of what was once even nominal Christian culture. I believe we are witnessing vivid aspects of this phenomenon in our western 'Christian' cultures today. It is said there is a suburb of a north of England town with a population of about 4,000 where only around 1% are white British, the rest being Muslims mostly from Pakistan. In saying this there is not a 'racist' thought in my mind because I know the kingdom of God as pictured in Revelation 7:9 is without distinction of race or language. It is only in the gospel of Christ that there is ever true racial harmony because in Christ there are no distinctions of a physical, racial, linguistic or gender type (Ephesians 2:19, 20; Galatians 3:28). But even 200 years ago, nobody living in Britain could have envisaged the fulfilment of the symbolism of the sixth trumpet as we see it today. The same applies to other once nominally Christian societies.

The impact is pain and death on a scale not seen before. The opened seals killed a quarter, this trumpet kills a third. Whether this has yet come to fruition in any respect I cannot tell, but I do know this world is ripe for God's judgment to fall. As it was in the days of Noah, so it is today (Luke 17:26-30). But despite the warnings and signs, mankind continues unrepentant. Verses 20 and 21 describe the idolatrous worship of mankind outside of Christ. Their continual breaking of the first and second tables of the law goes on unabated. Those commands relating to God's worship and the rest relating to living with one another. Just as

---

[8] Many references in scripture speak of war as a fire; see Hoeksema, *Behold He Cometh* on this passage.

77

Paul wrote in Romans chapter 1, there is no fear of God before their eyes. But then, as with the world of Noah's day and the area around Sodom, just when everyone in their rejection of God thought everything would continue as it had thus far, judgment fell and consumed them all.

This sixth trumpet, the second woe, speaks clearly of final judgment about to fall. I believe the signs are clearly to be seen. Fifty years ago in my teens I would have dismissed this as fanciful nonsense about as credible as Tolkien's *Lord Of The Rings*, but today we see it happening before our eyes. The momentous changes of even the last 30 years with instantaneous, borderless, internet communications and freedom of international movement declare that judgment is ripe. The precise timing is unknown to us but it is definitely set to fall. The key question is, are you ready? Are you hiding in Christ, or will you stubbornly continue in your rejection of the gospel?

Chapter 11

The Angel With The Little Book

Revelation 10

The book of Revelation is given by God to John to show his elect people how he will bring to complete fulfilment the implementation of his glorious kingdom of eternal bliss, peace and righteousness. It is given to show his servants how the whole of history, the rising and falling of great empires, cultures and societies, is all the outworking of the conflict between God and Satan. But it is also given with the assurance to God's people that there is never a moment when God is not in absolute, supreme control of everything. The events of history, the great calamities of war and natural disaster, though painful and alarming in so many ways, can in no way affect the eternal safety of those who are redeemed by the blood of Christ.

Six seals of the seven-sealed book are now open showing us six elements in God's plan to overthrow Satan's kingdom. Into this sin-cursed world God sent the gospel, but he sent also war, socio-economic strife and death. In the fifth and sixth seals he showed us the perpetual state of conflict between the kingdom of Satan and the church of Christ, and increasing portents of cataclysm in the universe announcing the approach of the end of this created order. Then, the seventh seal opened loosing seven angels with trumpets to blow; these are trumpets of judgment. The first four of them are all things focused on harming the earth as an environment capable of sustaining healthy life. The last three trumpets are announced as 'woes' because their effect is more spiritually serious than the first four trumpets.

The fifth trumpet, the first woe, is a plague of alluring, demonic, locusts with scorpions' tails which 'hurt' those men who have not God's seal on their foreheads. We saw that this plague represents the spirit of the age in which we live; godless, materialistic, unbelieving, morally deviant. Of course, this is as fallen mankind has always been but with an intensity that seems to be increasing dramatically with the burgeoning

79

world population. The sixth trumpet, the second woe, released a huge army of fearsome horsemen ushered in by the removal of ancient borders, whose effect is the death of a third of mankind, but despite this, the remainder of people continue in unrepentant law-breaking.

It is worth underlining the key principles of this second woe before we see why the vision of Revelation 10 was given.

The Second Woe
Today is just as it was in the days of Noah; everything is ripe for judgment. Who can plumb the depths to which mankind can sink in violating the two tables of God's law? In both man's relationship to God and the relationship of men to one another, God's precepts are flaunted and ignored. God's indictment of the sinfulness of man in the days of Noah, followed by the description of Sodom and Gomorrah in Paul's summary of first century society, from Romans chapter 1, is comparable with what we see today. The only difference is that today man's wickedness seems to be increasing in intensity and depravity. There is indeed 'no fear of God before their eyes'. Everyone seems to think they have a secure future after death, whether it be what is to some the comfort of annihilation or to others an imaginary heaven based on their personal self-righteousness. Only one thing fits a sinner for heaven and that is the blood of Christ, yet that very blood is despised by mankind in general and 'trodden underfoot' (Hebrews 10:29).

A voice comes from the horns of the altar (Revelation 9:13) picturing the blood of the sacrifice which itself pictured the blood of Christ. The voice speaks peace to the redeemed, but vengeance to Satan's kingdom. The voice is like a two-edged sword, speaking peace and vengeance. Paul tells us the gospel is a savour of death unto death and of life unto life (2 Corinthians 2:16). The sixth trumpet initiates God's end-time judgment of the kingdom of Satan just as in the time of the flood and at Sodom. Look at the signs of the times and acknowledge the end is approaching. I do not know when precisely, but I can say there has been rapid progress towards judgment in my lifetime. Much has changed in the world order symbolised by the seals and trumpets we have been considering.

The loosing of the four angels bound in Euphrates symbolises the removal of ancient borders between the outward kingdom of God or nominal Christendom, and the kingdoms with no gospel knowledge or influence, the kingdoms of Gog and Magog (Ezekiel 38). Has there not been a massive increase in the population of the non-Christianised world in the last few centuries? Consider the huge increase in international travel that has happened in the past 50 years. Consider what is pictured in the second woe as resulting from this removal of borders; war, desolation and pestilence. Has this woe already happened in some measure with the great conflicts of the 20th century? Perhaps a much greater conflict is yet to come. I cannot tell, but I do know that God will frustrate Satan's purposes, he will punish sin and he is in control of everything. The state of Utopia to which the world's politicians aspire will never be realised. Instead, God's word promises only the scorpion sting of Satanic delusion and the dreadful pain of human conflict and death. Furthermore, despite terrible judgment falling there will still be no repentance for murder, sorceries, fornication and theft (Revelation 9:21). The prospect appears alarming even for believers. The second woe sounds like a catalogue of judgments that will surely be dreadful to live through and cannot fail to touch everyone living including believers, as did the world wars of the 20th century. Therefore, God, in his infinite wisdom, has given his church Revelation chapter 10.

The Angel
In verse 1 of chapter 10, John tells us that he saw 'another mighty angel come down from heaven'. The way he is described as being adorned with rainbow, sun and pillars of fire, leaves little doubt but that this is the Lord Jesus Christ. The messenger or angel of the covenant is the Messiah (Malachi 3:1) and the fact that he came down from heaven chimes with the description of God, in the person of his Son, laying aside the glory of his heavenly position to come down to this earth (Philippians 2:5-11). He comes as a Prophet to manifest the unknowable God to his people but, supremely, as Redeemer to die in their place and cleanse them from sin. I think we can be confident that this mighty angel is Christ.

In the vision before us, he comes down holding a 'little book' and he stands with one foot on the earth and another in the sea. From that position he speaks out loudly in a way that cannot be ignored and in response, seven thunders speak. These are not just rumbles of thunder but words. It seems that John heard and understood the words for he was about to write them down when he was told not to do so yet. Then, on the authority of God who is supreme over all, we hear the angel announce that there should be time no more. The end is coming!

The mighty angel then declares that the seventh angel is yet to sound his trumpet which announces the unfolding of the end of all things in this created order. All God has revealed to his prophets will be fulfilled! Now John is commanded to go and take the little book from the hand of the angel. But when it is given to him, the angel says he must eat it up. The chapter concludes with a command to John to prophesy to many peoples, nations, tongues and kings. Let us look at what these things could signify.

The Little Book
Some say this is the same book, the seven-sealed book, we saw in Revelation 5:1, but that was a book whereas this is specified to be a little book. In what respect is this book little? It seems to me most plausible that its littleness is to be seen in its being an extract from the seven-sealed book. It contains what can be revealed to God's believing people of how the end will come, how the kingdom of Christ will finally triumph. It certainly contains the written word of God because verse 7 speaks of the 'mystery of God ... declared to the prophets'. Paul speaks more than once about the mystery God has revealed and he clearly means the gospel of Christ, the central focus of the entire Bible. I think, therefore, it is reasonable to assume the little book is at least the written word of God, and so it is itself the book of Revelation and certainly the portion as yet to be unfolded. Surely the loud voice of verse 3 and the seven thunders are speaking the message of the little book.

As already noted, John must have heard the message and understood it plainly for he was about to write it down. Why is he told not to write it down? I think, from what follows concerning eating the little book, we are to understand John's personal interest and involvement in the message. The implication here is that one cannot passively convey the message of the book as a disinterested bystander. Note the difference between 'disinterested' and 'uninterested'. I could attend the reading of a will as a disinterested party whilst being very interested in the contents of the will. As a disinterested party I know the will leaves nothing to me personally, but I may nevertheless be very interested to know what it says! When it comes to the contents of the little book do you think of yourself as a disinterested party? Are you merely intrigued by the book of Revelation as a piece of ancient literature? Are you fascinated by the genre and the way other, secular, literature attempts to mimic its style and visions? Or do you know that, along with everyone else, you are most definitely an interested party in its reading, for none shall escape the end of all things, the certainty of judgment, and the coming kingdom of God?

If the contents must not be revealed just yet, what can we learn from the angel's pronouncement? In verses 5 and 6 he swears by God, creator of all things, because he can swear by none higher (Hebrews 6:13). His message is there should be time no longer; he is announcing the impending end of all things. At the point of this announcement, the end is imminent and looming but it is not now, because the seventh angel has yet to sound his trumpet. At that stage the 'mystery of God should be finished'. Everything God's servants the prophets have declared of the gospel and the coming of Christ's kingdom will be fulfilled, but the details of the end will be opened up only when the seventh trumpet actually sounds.

Eating The Little Book

Eating the little book is reinforcing the idea you cannot be impartial about the message of the little book. John is told to go to the angel and get the little book, and not just the book but its message. The instruction to John to eat it symbolises the need for its message to become part of him to such an extent that he must preach it. When the flood was approaching in Noah's day, the burden of the message of coming judgment was laid upon Noah so that as well as building an ark, picturing Christ as the one and only way of salvation, Noah also preached. Thus burdened he had to preach the message and over many years, while an unbelieving world poured scorn on him, Noah was a preacher of righteousness (2 Peter 2:5).

When John ate the little book it was sweet in his mouth but bitter in his stomach. The gospel message of salvation, the message of the triumph of God's kingdom, is sweet in the mouth. To the one burdened and heavy-laden with sin before God, the invitation to come to Christ for rest is sweet, indeed. More than that, how sweet is the experience of it? Sweeter also than honey and the honeycomb (Psalm 19:10). But the bitterness comes as a consequence of the incompatibility of spiritual things and carnal things. There is contradiction from the world to the believer imbibing the sweet gospel message. My wife and I love choral singing but recently we had to drop out of rehearsals because, believing the sweetness of the true gospel, we simply could not sing the Catholic heresy of Elgar's 'Dream of Gerontius' despite the musical arrangement being the Mount Everest of choral works. That was bitter to do but we could not continue with it.

Finally, in verse 11, we see the reason for his needing to eat the little book. He has to go and preach its message to many people, without distinction of race, language or social status. How else shall they hear unless a preacher is sent to them? (Romans 10:12-17). This is God's way. By the foolishness of preaching God calls out his lost sheep. He calls them into the safety of the ark, which is Christ, before the end comes. The message of the little book is the gospel of Christ. It is the message of redemption accomplished by the shedding of Christ's precious blood for the people of God's sovereign choice. But the climax of the gospel is the end of this world, the overthrow of Satan's kingdom and the arrival of the redeemed in eternal glory. The little book will reveal how these things shall unfold as we progress through the rest of Revelation.

Application

Think for a moment about the way you relate to this world. Momentous things are going on all the time. If you are an unbeliever this world is your only hope, it is all you have to hope in and really it is no hope at all. You need to heed the warnings of scripture and flee from the wrath that is surely to come. Flee to the only place of safety, the only 'ark of safety'. Flee to Christ.

If you are a believer you are in the world at God's behest; note you are in it but not of it. Seek the wisdom of God to use your time here wisely, enjoy the good, avoid the bad, live responsibly and soberly in it. Be guided by the gospel precepts of God's word, but always remember whose you are and whom you serve, whose side you are on and your final destiny. Remember what you were and where God has put you in Christ. Meditate on the spiritual blessings you have in him and be prepared to stand for Christ whatever might arise. He is in control. Did you notice immediately following the dreadful details of the sixth trumpet we are comforted with the picture of Christ standing in the sea and on the earth? He is in supreme control of everything and so nothing, not even the most severe of the judgments that are to fall, can stop Christ's saints from reaching heaven.

Determine to stand fast with Joshua, "Choose you this day whom you will serve, but as for me and my house, we will serve the Lord" (Joshua 24:15).

Chapter 12

God's Two Witnesses

Revelation 11:1-13

The account of the opening of the seals and the blowing of the trumpets of judgment, though written over 1900 years ago, accurately portrays our 21st century society in so many ways. The judgment of God is being witnessed all around the world. If you believe Christ you are comforted to know you are immune from the scorpion-like sting of the locusts, and because Christ controls all things, even those aspects of judgment that may physically touch you cannot hurt you spiritually. The remainder of the seven-sealed book will now be implemented. This was referred to in Revelation 10:7. The seventh angel must sound out concerning the end of this space-time creation. The end of this world and the end of the kingdom of Satan is coming. The only escape is by the blood of the Lamb. Noah preached righteousness before the flood, God's prophets, his preachers, must unrelentingly preach the gospel right up to the end, warning of judgment to come. This was the command at the end of chapter 10. Throughout what remains of this world, God's people will know the sweetness of gospel salvation and the bitterness of enmity with the unbelieving world.

Who Must Preach And Witness?
Revelation 11 opens with a picture of John being given a measuring rod with which to measure or mark out the temple. Strange as this may seem, I think it helps clear up some confusion that may have arisen in previous chapters, especially concerning the sixth trumpet or second woe. In that vision the four angels bound in the great river Euphrates were loosed and this opened the way for a 200 million strong army of fearsome horsemen to bring about the death of a third of mankind. We interpreted this as the countries of the world of a Judeo-Christian heritage, sometimes called Christendom, being overrun by the kingdoms of Gog and Magog, or the peoples who have never had any cultural influence from the gospel.

I suggested this was Christendom being overrun from without by non-Christendom. But knowing what we believe concerning the true gospel and its narrow distinctiveness, you might have been puzzled as to why I gave any significance at all to the religious system of rituals and traditions called 'Christendom'. After all, fast-forwarding to Revelation 17 and 18, we see most of Christendom being marked out in the sight of God as spiritually-wicked Babylon. In those chapters, what at first looks like the church of Christ, represented by a woman, is in fact revealed as a 'whore' who denies gospel truth to its very heart. Nevertheless, there are swathes of what we identify as 'western culture' for example, Europe, the Americas, Australia and other places, which claim, at least nominally to be 'Christian'. Whether they be Eastern Orthodox, Roman Catholic, Episcopalian, Protestant and even Reformed, they can all be traced back to the opening of the first seal, the sending forth of the White Horse of the gospel into the world. In frustrating Satan's purposes, the White Horse has not only been calling out God's true elect from every tribe and kindred, but inspiring a huge amount of nominal Christianity ultimately to be revealed as false religion and called 'Babylon'.

Many claim to be God's true witnesses in this world. My wife and I recently visited Rome and marvelled at the magnificence of over two millennia of history; ancient architecture and stunning works of art. But on every side we were confronted with the claims of the Roman Catholic Church to be the true witness of God on earth. This raises the question of whether it is possible to mark out the true church of Christ from Babylon waiting to be revealed. I believe the Bible says we can and Revelation 11:1, 2 tells us what it is that marks out Christ's true witness from merely nominal Christianity, or Christendom, and ultimately Babylon.

As if in answer to the question of who are called to preach God's truth and who, in addition to John, might be included in the 'Thou' of Revelation 10:11, we are given Revelation 11.

John is told only to measure, to mark out, the core of the temple but not to measure the outer court nor the rest of the city of Jerusalem. Remember this is symbolical, it is not speaking of literal Jerusalem. Here, 'Jerusalem' pictures Christendom but only the core of the temple signifies the true people of God. The court is given over to the Gentiles, that is, those who are not the Israel of God (Galatians 6:16). These spiritual Gentiles 'tread the holy city underfoot for 42 months'. They are in the vicinity of the true people of God, but they are not themselves his people. They are men whose spiritual number is six that is, short of God's perfect seven, but who are striving to grasp perfection and achieve divinity and so it is for 6x7=42 months that they tread down the Lord's true people. I do not claim to understand anything approaching the full depth of this symbolism but I cannot help noticing it. God's Spirit has put the words here for us to read, hear and keep (Revelation 1:3).

Let us consider the nature of the 'marking out' between wider Christendom and the true church of Christ. The numbers comprising Christendom must run into billions[9], but 144,000 symbolises[10] the true people of God on earth at any time in history. The clearest line of all between the true and the counterfeit people of God is that all but Christ's true people deny the efficacy of Christ's blood as the sole means of salvation. They all deny that 'Jesus Christ is come in the flesh' (1 John 4:1) meaning they deny that all the Old Testament said of the Messiah and the salvation of his particular people is fulfilled in the person and work of Jesus of Nazareth. These deniers of Jesus Christ are widely regarded as Christian by, for example, politicians and the media, but in reality they epitomise the treading of the holy city underfoot by those who deny the gospel. Apply the test as John instructs us in his first epistle. Yes, they agree a man walked this earth called Jesus of Nazareth but they deny what God has revealed of his saving work and its extent.

Beyond what is obviously false, look at those who profess to be true gospel believers. In saying this I am not calling for a negative, judgmental spirit, yet true believers are called to be discerning. Today, many churches profess to uphold the true gospel but in reality deny it by compromising primary doctrine, tolerating false teaching and associating with the doctrines and practices of heresy. Even churches that only a few years ago stood solidly for Bible truth are now compromised with liberal practices. The old waymarks have been removed. In effect they deny the gospel truth of salvation by grace alone, through faith alone, in Christ alone. They adopt free-will methods of evangelism on the one hand and add the bondage of law-works on the other. Whatever they might claim to be they are not within the temple which John is directed to measure.

A further mark of distinction is that the true church is distinguished from the false by the ministry gifts God has given to it. God's ministry gifts cause his true believing people to experience the sweetness of the gospel and rejoice in it (Philippians 3:3), while bearing the bitterness of

---

[9] The Roman Catholic Church alone claims to have about 1.2 billion adherents.

[10] It would not surprise me, if it is so revealed in heaven, to discover that 144,000 was the *actual number* of true believers in the world on 5th November 2016, today's date.

their clash with the world and false religion. God's ministry gifts do not place his people under bondage to law in any respect.

The True Church Pictured By The Temple

The New Testament makes explicit what is implicit in the Old Testament. 1 Corinthians 3:16, 17 and 2 Corinthians 6:16, 17 describe the church, believers, as the temple of God. Ephesians 2:21 pictures individual believers as building stones forming the temple of God. 1 Peter 2:5-9 continues the theme of Ephesians in describing believers as living stones built into a 'spiritual house' and also as the priests within the temple. Whatever the rest of the religious world thinks of itself, this is the true spiritual temple of God. Philippians 3:3 reinforces the identification of the true people of God, in contrast to the merely religious, as those who worship God in the spirit, rejoice in Christ Jesus and have no confidence in the flesh.

The Old Testament rebuilding of the temple after the Babylonian exile was undertaken in the face of extreme worldly opposition and pictures the true New Testament church as it is today. The details are given in Haggai, Zechariah and Ezra. Zerubbabel and Joshua are prince and priest in the venture giving light to God's people and sustained by Holy Spirit oil with the assurance that 'not by might, nor by power, but by my spirit saith the Lord of hosts' (Zechariah 4:6). They stand as two witnesses in those Old Testament days. What could be taken as 'two witnesses' in these New Testament days? It seems to me the two witnesses of Revelation 11 are first, the members of the true church of Christ, and second, the church's true ministers. I am aware that many identify the Revelation 11 witnesses as literally Moses and Elijah from verse 6 because of the physical manifestations of God's power they call forth, Moses with plagues in Egypt and Elijah with a 3½ year drought. However, I am confident these men are cited as types of all of God's true witnesses in this world.

What Must They Testify?

Verse 4 speaks of the oil of God's grace and it is of God's grace they must be witnesses. They declare gospel righteousness, redemption accomplished in Christ's blood, sinners freely justified and the wrath of judgment turned away. This is the focus of the witnesses' testimony, the gospel of God's redeeming love. I challenge every church that 'has a name that it is alive' (Revelation 3:1) to declare honestly whether the overwhelming core of their message is the gospel of sovereign grace, and particular redemption by the precious blood of Jesus Christ alone. Without that everything else they might say is mere empty words.

Complementary to the central gospel message, must be warning of impending judgment, as surely as Noah warned his generation. Verse 3 speaks of sackcloth which throughout scripture symbolises repentance. Repentance in hope of escaping judgment. Sackcloth also indicates the need to deliver the testimony without any of the trappings, allurements or gimmicks of the world. How sad to see once faithful churches increasingly adopting worldly techniques and methods to make the message they preach more appealing to the natural flesh of man.

Verse 5 tells of fire proceeding from the witnesses' mouths in response to worldly attack. This echoes God's promise through Jeremiah that he would make the prophet's words as fire in his mouth if delivered faithfully according to the truth of God (Jeremiah 5:14). The 'fire' is judgment declared as the certain end for rejecting the gospel. The two witnesses, Christ's church and his anointed preachers, proclaim these things in the face of opposition, scorn, and unbelief using only spiritual weapons (2 Corinthians 10:4), but these are 'mighty through God to the pulling down of strongholds'. With their words they will 'kill' (v. 5), they will silence the power of those who oppose the message, and they will bring down God's judgments on this kingdom of Satan as did Noah, Moses, Elijah, Zerubbabel and Joshua the priest.

For How Long?

Revelation 11 is a high-level summary of how the end comes with much more detail to be revealed in later chapters.

Verse 3 states that the prophesying of the two witnesses will be for 1,260 days, until they have finished their testimony (v. 7). They will prophesy until the end is imminent, until God by these two witnesses has said everything he must say both to call his elect to himself and warn of impending judgment. And how are we to understand 1,260 days?

Please bear with some more Biblical numerics. 1,260 days is 42 months (if a month is 30 days). 42 months is 3½ years of 12 months (if a year is 360 days as in the number of degrees in a circle) and this can be read as 'a time, times and half a time'. Twice 3½ is seven, God's number of perfection. Six is the number of the beast and of man, i.e. one less than the seven of God's perfection. Six multiplying seven gives 42 (see v. 2), the number of months that the spiritual Gentiles shall tread underfoot the holy city. That is fallen man's best attempt to make perfection in Satan's kingdom and it results in failure. So the 1,260 days of the witnesses' prophesying is the same as the 42 months or 3½ years of Satan's kingdom striving but failing to achieve perfection without the justice of God. It is the time from Christ's ascension to his return at the end of all things; it is symbolically half of the perfect duration of God's creation which must be seven. I have already said that I do not fully understand the depths of meaning in these numbers, but there is surely great significance in them. I am not advocating the sort of nonsense peddled in many books on Revelation. How then do we bring our thoughts and understanding back to some sort of tangible reality?

A 'time' is a long time, 'times' is twice as long; those living through these times must think they are never going to end. But then the next 'time' is cut short half way through just when most people think it is going to continue as the preceding 'times' have done. This is the symbolical 3½ years, the 1,260 days, the time we are now living in from Christ's ascension to his return. It is a long time but a limited time. What are God's believing people called to do? They are called to witness, to be ready always to give a reason for the hope that is in them to anyone who asks them (1 Peter 3:15), and the church's preachers are called to preach the gospel, calling sinners to Christ and warning of the certainty of judgment. They are to strive to grow in grace and the knowledge of Christ, to bear opposition with patience and to increase in their hope for eternal glory in Christ.

What To Expect

In the light of these things, having a measure of understanding of what God has revealed through John concerning his true church and wider Christendom in these days, what can we expect to happen next?

Above all else we can be confident that God will keep his people; Christ prayed for this and it will surely be granted (John 17:11, 15). Living in the world but not of the world, Christ's church will be kept in wilderness separation from the principles of the world and will be fed by God (Revelation 12:6) until they are all taken to glory (Revelation 11:12). But that will not happen before their testimony is to all intents and purposes silenced (v. 7).

The beast of verse 7 is Satan's Antichrist which we shall see in greater clarity in later chapters. For now suffice it to say that Antichrist is manifested in all false religion and all self-righteous attempts to reach heaven without the Christ of God. This beast ascends from the bottomless pit (v. 7), makes war on God's two witnesses, overcomes them and kills them. The witnesses' dead bodies lie unburied in the street of the world's 'city', the metropolis of peoples that reject the true God. Symbolically,

90

and spiritually, this city is Sodom, it is Egypt, it is even Jerusalem where our Lord was crucified, it is the God-rejecting, gospel-rejecting, world we see all around us today. And seeing the witnesses' bodies lying openly in the street, the world's people refuse to let them be buried out of sight. They go so far (v. 10) as celebrating the death of the witnesses because the message of grace and warning that so tormented them has been silenced, seemingly forever. Their sin can now progress without restraint, or so they think.

We are speaking of a time when the true church and its ministers are effectively silenced, disrupted and made to be non-functioning as living, visible, churches bearing God's testimony. It is my conviction that in the UK today the church which stands solidly for the true gospel is as good as 'lying dead in the street'. Even 30 years ago, you could find churches ministering the gospel of free sovereign grace widely distributed. Today you struggle to find a handful remaining true. Even where the witness is upheld, it is often the case that the fellowships concerned are unable to function as a living church with building, structure, a good number of members and a visible life as a church. That is the case with our own gathering. Here in the UK we meet in a home on Sunday mornings only, with barely ten adults meeting together. To the world and false religion we are 'lying dead in the street'. Even when we had a regular meeting place, Satan's beast contrived to make it practically impossible for us to hold public meetings there throughout the 9-month rugby football season! Even in the USA where there is a thriving association of independent free grace churches and pastors[11], the numbers involved are miniscule compared to the population of the country and the populous swathes of Arminian, Catholic, Episcopalian, Reformed and Presbyterian churches claiming to represent modern 'Christianity'. I believe we are living in the days described here in Revelation 11:7-10.

Nevertheless, these are exciting days! The signs of Christ's return are increasing. Who would have thought 30 years ago that Revelation 11:7-10 would be happening as I have described here? What God signified through John over 1,900 years ago is unfolding unmistakeably as prophesied then. Not only that, the death of the witnesses is only as it appears to the world and false religion. The true church of Christ will never really die. The gates of hell shall not prevail against it! Look at verse 11; after just 3½ days lying apparently dead the witnesses stand up and great fear falls on all.

---

[11] Many whose messages are available at www.freegraceradio.com

While the world and false religion is rejoicing over the demise of what it recognises as functioning witnesses for God, the gospel has never been more clearly preached than it is in these days. I consider it remarkable that co-incident with the demise of what was the visible witness of God in the world, let us call it faithful evangelical churches preaching sovereign grace in most towns throughout the country, the internet has blossomed. Especially in the last 15 years there has been a quite unexpected facility and ability for 'scattered sheep' to join others for worship and to hear the gospel faithfully and powerfully preached. Our own little group of 10 or so is now joined by possibly hundreds of others around the world using the internet. As verse 11 says, there is cause for the world and false religion to fear. You see, the witnesses are not dead; they are brimming with the life of Christ and shortly they shall hear that blessed voice of verse 12 declare, "Come up hither!". The day of the Lord is surely close (1 Thessalonians 5:2). Are you living on the 'tiptoe of faith' looking for the blessed hope and glorious appearing of the Great God our Saviour, Jesus Christ?

Chapter 13

A Summary Of The End

Revelation 11:7-19

Revelation 11 brings us to the end of the third of the seven visions of the whole book. This vision focuses on the blowing of the seven trumpets of judgment whilst assuring God's people their prayers for the coming of God's kingdom are heard. It reminds us the judgments of this world are under Christ's complete control. Whatever the Lord's people are called to live through, their wellbeing is guaranteed and they will certainly all be taken up into heaven. At the end of this vision we have what seems like a management summary of the remainder of Revelation concerning the end of all things and this is consistent with the idea of the little book of Revelation 10. For anyone who has worked in business, producing reports and proposals, the management summary is very important. It is provided to help busy executives readily understand the context, the key issues, the proposed solution, etc., without having to read all of the detail. This is what we seem to have towards the end of Revelation 11.

Remember again how we got to this point.[12] Seals and trumpets have been sent by God into this world to frustrate Satan's intention of establishing his kingdom. His is a kingdom of false peace and imitation righteousness giving false hope of some sort of eternal good. The seals consisted in the following manifestations: the gospel sent out into Satan's kingdom, war between nations, socio-economic strife, death, conflict between Satan and the church, portents of cosmic cataclysm, then the seventh seal opened as seven trumpets. The first four trumpets all seem

---

[12] I am conscious of often repeating the development of our understanding of Revelation and readers might wonder why I do not leave it to individuals to re-read previous chapters, but each chapter is intended to reflect a specific sermon and is based closely on my sermon notes. Each chapter as such needs to stand alone in its message and ministry to its readers/hearers. I beg the reader's indulgence to bear with me even if some aspects seem somewhat repetitious.

93

designed to harm the earth's ability to sustain healthy life. Then three woes are pronounced. The first woe unfolds as a plague of demonic locusts, symbolising the depravity of all aspects of human existence without Christ, be it human philosophy, science, morality or aspirations. The second woe indicates war, desolation and pestilence arising from the removal of ancient borders, nevertheless, there is no repentance of men in general. This tells us not to expect a general conversion to Christ before the end, as many like to suggest.

In the midst of a symbolical 'holy city' that we might call Christendom, John has measured out the only true dwelling place of God and that is the temple at the city's core. Not even the temple court was to be measured as it is 'given to the Gentiles', and the rest of the 'holy city' was to be left to be trodden underfoot by them. This helped us to narrowly mark out the 144,000 which God counts as his true believing people in contrast to the billions that constitute wider Christendom. Thus narrowed down, God's two witnesses, meaning his believing people and their God-ordained ministers, are to continue to the end to testify of the certainty of judgment and the gospel as the only way of escape.

The End
People generally pour scorn on the idea of the coming end of the world and of divine judgment falling. Indeed, 2 Peter 3:3, 4 accurately summarizes the views of most people today. Peter warns they will ignore the lessons of Noah's day when everybody thought the same and were all, in a day, swept away in the flood. Today's science, much of it falsely so-called (1 Timothy 6:20), accepts the idea of a beginning of this space-time universe, a 'Big Bang', and acknowledges the mathematics of it strongly suggests a return to a similar 'singularity'. In other words an end, though according to models of stellar evolution not for another five billion years. But the Book of God insists upon it, the end of all things is coming and coming soon. In Revelation 10:6 we hear Christ declaring on the highest authority there should be 'time no longer'. How do you react to that? I am talking just now primarily to those who claim to believe the gospel and to follow Christ. Do you fear for what you will lose? Lot's wife looked back to Sodom where her heart truly was. Or do you hope for the speedy end of all things, the end of this sin-cursed world, and all of its troubles? Our personal troubles surely increase with bodily ageing. The world rejoices in the benefits of more people living longer; yet as I observe my own father, aged 91, living in a nursing home with no mobility, all of his mental capacities intact but effectively confined as a prisoner to his room, it seems to me a 'benefit' I could happily forgo.

Should not the believer's attitude to the end of all things be the same as Paul's in Philippians 1:21-24? He longed for Christ to take him to glory out of this world, yet was content to stay as long as the Lord willed in order to serve Christ's cause and minister to his people. It is a good test of our priorities regularly to apply this to ourselves.

Believers' Prospects
We have seen that believers are assured of God's omnipotent protection. We will most certainly be called up to heaven to join God's innumerable multitude in eternal bliss and perfection (Revelation 11:12). But before we go our testimony as churches and preachers will appear to the world and false religion to be silenced. Satan's false religion promotes mankind's self-righteous efforts to secure peace and reach 'heaven' without the satisfaction of divine justice. It hates the preaching of Christ's blood atonement. Opposition from Antichrist will leave the two witnesses lying dead and unburied in the street, effectively silenced, disrupted and non-functioning as living churches in the eyes of the world. But God's true church is never overcome. Just as the witnesses stand on their feet (v. 11) true believers are enabled, graciously and providentially, to have fellowship with each other, and hear the gospel faithfully preached, for example via the internet, until the call comes for them to be taken up to glory. We watch and wait for the blessed hope and glorious appearing of our precious Saviour Jesus Christ.

In contrast with the believer's hope and expectation, what is going ultimately to become of this world?

The Seventh Trumpet Or The Third Woe
In Revelation 11:15 the seventh angel sounds his trumpet. In the verses following it is announced as already accomplished that God's kingdom is finally realised in unchallenged supremacy, and the prayer of God's people is fulfilled.

In this world now God is sovereign but his sovereignty is constantly challenged by Satan and his kingdom of darkness and lies. Think back to Genesis 1 and 2. In the beginning God created the world perfect and without sin. He put it under the rule of Adam as his viceroy. But in the Fall, Adam subjected himself, all his race and the kingdom of this world to the prince of darkness. It has continued so ever since but now the seventh trumpet sounds. The end of that order is announced.

The sounding of the trumpet prompts 'great voices in heaven'. I am told by those who know better than me that what they actually say is,

"The kingdom (singular) of this world is become the kingdom of our God and of his Christ and he shall reign for ever and ever." The kingdom of creation that Adam handed over to Satan's rule is restored to its rightful viceroy, the Lord Jesus Christ. He is the one who opens the seals and instigates the trumpets and at this stage in the vision he is seen as supremely victorious. Read 1 Corinthians 15:22-28 to see the eternal blessedness, true righteousness and glorious peace that is the lot of those who are found in Christ when the seventh trumpet sounds. Paul says in Romans 8:18, 'I reckon that the sufferings of this present time are not worthy to be compared with the glory which shall be revealed in us.'

Follow the verses of Revelation 11 down to the end of the chapter. In verse 16 all the redeemed give reverential worship to God. Everything we now experience of the seals being opened, the trumpets sounding, the pouring out of vials, of which we have yet to see the detail in later chapters, all of it is over and done with and the church is victorious in heaven. What a comfort to the church (v. 17) to experience consciously our great God taking to himself his great power and reigning in majesty. What worship it draws forth from the redeemed!

But look in verse 18; here is the management summary of the final judgment. There is much more detail to be unfolded as we progress towards the end of the Book of Revelation, but for now, this is the summary: the nations, the unbelieving, Christ-rejecting peoples of this world are furious. They are furious because the time of judgment has come, the wrath of God is going to fall on them, but also they are angry because they see God rewarding his servants; his prophets, his saints and them that fear his name. God's elect are blessed while destruction falls on the wicked for their rebellion and sin.

No doubt the nations find the prospect of reward for the saints to be unjust as they await their own just condemnation. It seems as if verse 19 is given in answer to their objection. The temple of God is opened in heaven. From an earthly perspective the temple represents the dwelling place of God with man symbolised by the tabernacle from the wilderness wanderings and by the actual building in Old Testament Jerusalem. This was where God had said he would dwell with his covenant people on earth. It pictures what we eventually see in Revelation 21 and 22 as the heavenly temple, heaven itself, where the redeemed spend eternity in the intimate presence of their God and Saviour. Is God unjust in taking them to that state of bliss whilst pouring out his wrath on the 'nations'? No! Look what is on display in the temple in heaven. It is the ark of his testament. The ark, is the box in the Old Testament tabernacle that contained the tablets of the law given at Sinai, a golden pot of the manna that fed Israel in the wilderness and Aaron's rod that budded, declaring the presence of the Spirit of God upon his anointed priest. Above it, as a covering, was the golden Mercy Seat with its overarching cherubim. There the blood of an acceptable sacrifice was sprinkled. The propitiating blood turned away God's wrath against sin because it satisfied offended justice. The sin-debt to the law is paid in full by the blood, but not the blood of animal sacrifices for they were themselves only pictures and types. No, the only blood that brings peace is the precious blood of Christ as of a Lamb without blemish and without spot. This declares, in response to accusations of injustice at God's grace, how God has remained perfectly just in saving and justifying the people of his choice (Isaiah 45:21; Romans 3:26; 9:14-16).

The lightning, voices, thunderings, earthquake and great hail all announce and summarise the judgments to follow in subduing all rebellion, confirming God reigns supreme in unchallenged sovereignty.

Conclusion
Believer, do you despair at the sorry state of the true church today compared with times past? Do you wring your hands at the increasing wickedness in world society? Do you see real hopelessness despite the optimism of political leaders? Young people, is this world where all your hopes and aspirations are founded? Those of you in middle-age, can you not hear the clock ticking, the years advancing? You elderly, do you not long for a better prospect than one of failing health and increasing dependency upon others? Hear what God clearly says and flee to Christ for refuge. The promise of God is eternal life, with God himself being the 'exceeding great reward' of his people in his triumphant kingdom of peace and righteousness. Oh, that our God would graciously give you a thirst for those heavenly things and make you willing in the day of his power to come to him.

Chapter 14

The War For The Kingdom

Revelation 12:1-12

Having seen an overview of the end of all things in the last half of Revelation 11, chapter 12 opens the fourth of the seven visions of the book. It is a vision of Christ and his church persecuted by Satan, world governments and false religion. In this chapter, God shows his people the conflict there has been from the Fall in Eden to the final judgment between God and Satan. A conflict for unrivalled supremacy over the kingdom God created. This vision was written over 1,900 years ago for our learning and comfort. We have been assured of the end result. Pay attention to these words and with the Holy Spirit's enabling you will see what has been going on, the reason for it, and you will learn to trust God more for you will see everything he has said is patently true.

Overview Of Revelation Chapter 12
The chapter divides clearly into three parts, first, verses1-6; second, verses 7-12; third, verses 13-17. It appears somewhat as a movie might or a novel with flashbacks interjected as the story unfolds. We see Lucifer's uprising, challenging God's rule and sovereignty, seeking to take over God's creation and enthral God's viceroy, Adam. We see him fighting God's redeemer and seeking to destroy him at birth. He makes war in heaven challenging the legality of the glorification of the Old Testament saints and then persecuting the New Testament church to mould it by force into conformity with the world which is his empire. Let us look at the first two sections of the chapter.

The Woman And The Dragon

John sees a 'great wonder in heaven'. The word 'wonder' suggests a sign to be looked upon. The sign is a woman clothed with the sun. This is the church, the elect people of God, the bride of Christ, the kingdom of God, the Shulamite of Solomon's song. 'Who is she that looketh forth as the morning, fair as the moon, clear as the sun?' (Song of Solomon 6:10). Ephesians 5:25-33 gives directions for human marriage but Paul says really it is a picture of the eternal marriage between Christ and his bride, the church. Note the woman's crown of twelve stars, surely the church in the world symbolised by twelve patriarchs and twelve apostles, twelve being three, the number of God, multiplying four, the number of the created world. The woman is pregnant, weak and vulnerable, bringing a child into the world (v. 2). Who could this child be?

In verse 5 we see he is a man-child who is to rule all nations with a rod of iron. Psalm 2 speaks poetically of this man-child. He is God's anointed, his king whom he sits on Mount Zion. He is God's Son to whom the Father gives the heathen for an inheritance. He is described here also as ruling all nations with a rod of iron. People are exhorted to 'kiss this Son' to avoid the certainty of God's wrath. Compare Revelation 2:27, Revelation 12:5 and Revelation 19:15 where we discover that a clear mark of Christ's identity is his rule with a rod of iron. This child being born of the woman is Christ.

But because the woman in the first two verses has not yet given birth to the man-child, she pictures the Old Testament church, the spiritual line promised to Adam and Eve whence the promised Seed of the woman would come to crush Satan's head (Genesis 3:15).

In verses 3 and 4 we see the red dragon. He is warlike, he has seven heads by which he tries to mimic God's number of perfection and ten horns symbolising complete earthly power. His crowns symbolise his rule as prince of the power of the air (Ephesians 2:2). In his rebellion against God he brings a third of the stars, the angels, with him making them into demons in his cause. This is clearly Satan and that is confirmed when we get to verse 9 where the dragon is identified. Immediately following the Fall in Eden, Satan heard the promise of God that the Seed of the woman would come to crush his head. He did not know how but he must endeavour to stop the Seed from coming and try to thwart his plans. If he cannot manage to stop the Seed from coming, he will try his best to kill the Seed as soon as he comes. He stands before the woman to devour the child as soon as it is born (v. 4). He spends the time from the Fall to Christ's birth watching, waiting and scheming the destruction of the Seed.

Eve gave birth to Cain and thought he was the promised Seed. She said, 'I have gotten a man from the Lord'. But Cain was godless and denied the only thing that could satisfy God's offended justice. Cain brought his own works as an offering to God when only the blood of the promised Seed could make satisfaction. Eve had already borne Abel who is godly and demonstrates an understanding of grace by bringing a lamb to God. Satan prompts Cain to kill Abel thinking perhaps that he, Abel, was the promised Seed. Satan then goes on trying to compromise the godly line of descendants by enticing the 'sons of God' to inter-marry with the 'daughters of men'. This continues up to the flood when God's promised judgment falls on sin and everyone is swept away except Noah and his family through whom God saves the promised Seed in the ark. At Babel, under the leadership of the great rebel, Nimrod, Satan tries to strengthen his kingdom of Christ-less satisfaction of divine justice. The people build the tower of Babel, reaching for heaven on their own terms. Here we see a world united in language and purpose to achieve Satan's aims and reject the Christ of God. But God divides their speech into mutually incomprehensible languages and thus establishes nation states. Doing so he loosed the second seal and the red horse of war came into Satan's kingdom. The world-wide Christ-less unity he had been engineering was thwarted.

Then we read of Abraham being called out of worldly idolatry and receiving God's promise that from his seed God would establish the promised Seed of Genesis 3:15. Abraham and Sarah were well past the age of bearing children but Abraham believed God. Did Abraham think 'his only Isaac' was the promised Seed? Did Satan scheme Mount Moriah would be the end of the Seed? We could go on through all of the Old Testament, through Jacob, Joseph, and Israel in Egypt and the Satanic oppression that happened there. What was Pharaoh's direction to kill all of the Israelites' male children other than Satan's attempt to destroy the promised Seed? In the wilderness wanderings Satan afflicted Israel with apostasy, warred against them with enemies, seduced them with idolatry and so it goes on throughout their history until he thinks he has destroyed them in the Babylonian captivity. But Cyrus is God's instrument for deliverance. The temple is rebuilt, its sacrifices picturing redemption are restored and the remnant 'seed' continues looking for the promise of the Seed. Antiochus Epiphanes inflicts cruel persecution on the Jews killing many of the 'woman's seed' and stops the daily temple sacrifice but he can never quite achieve his ultimate objective.

Then, when the 'fulness of the time is come' (Galatians 4:4) the promised Seed is born, made of a woman, made under the law to redeem his people from the curse of sin (Galatians 3:13). From the Fall this 'fulness of the time' would be a 'time, times and half a time' (3½), in other words 'half way through' the duration of this space-time creation which must be represented by God's perfect seven. His birth fulfilled all God's promises concerning his coming despite Satan's opposition. He was born of a virgin (Isaiah 7:14) in Bethlehem of Judaea (Micah 5:2). As an infant, Satan tried to have him killed by Herod; as a man engaged in his earthly ministry he tried to kill him using the Pharisees and the rule of Rome. At the cross he must have been triumphant, thinking finally he had destroyed the promised Seed. However, as Peter preached to the crowd in Jerusalem on the Day of Pentecost (Acts 2:23, 24) it was all in accordance with God's purposes of salvation. Christ's death made satisfaction to the law for the sins of his elect; God remained just and justifier of each and every one of them. In this way God qualified his elect for heavenly citizenship (Colossians 1:12). Satan, the strong man of the house, who had sought to destroy the promised Seed was himself bound so his goods might be plundered (Matthew 12:29). Being bound he was disarmed.

In verse 10 he is called the 'accuser of our brethren' but Satan's accusations are found to be without basis because of the death of Christ, as Romans 8:33, 34 confirms, 'Who shall lay any thing to the charge of God's elect? It is God that justifieth. Who is he that condemneth? It is Christ that died, yea rather, that is risen again, who is even at the right hand of God, who also maketh intercession for us.'

With salvation accomplished, the child (Revelation 12:5) is caught up to heaven to his throne. Our Lord Jesus Christ rose from the dead vindicated in his sacrifice for his people's sins and triumphant over Satan whose head he has effectively crushed. What then, is the war in heaven about (v. 7)? Here we have a flashback or a different perspective on the same facts we have been observing. There is a lot more to say concerning verse 6 and the woman in the wilderness for 1,260 days, but we will come back to that later. For now let us conclude this chapter with a look at the heavenly war of verses 7-12.

The Heavenly War

Since the Fall in Eden there had been war in heaven. Satan had been constantly accusing Old Testament saints (v. 10) of being unqualified for heaven because he could not see how God's promised Seed could make satisfaction for the sins of those already taken to heaven. For example,

102

Enoch did not experience death and was taken directly to heaven even though he was of Adam's race. How was that possible? Satan would bring the sin of the Old Testament saints before the bar of divine justice and scream for their eviction from heaven into his kingdom. But Michael and his angels fight with him. Some whom I respect greatly take Michael here to be Christ but I cannot agree with that. Michael is the chief of the angels of God fighting with Satan and his fallen angels. In Daniel 10:13 the man of Daniel's vision is plainly Christ, but Christ says that Michael came to help him in an endeavour against Satan. Michael and his angels fight with Satan and his demons. Let us enquire as to the nature of the fight.

I believe Michael is arguing, with the same weapons of warfare Paul refers to in 2 Corinthians 10:4. He argues that though he has not yet died in time, Christ is the Lamb slain from the foundation of the world (Revelation 13:8). As soon as Christ has died, has satisfied justice, risen from the dead and ascended to glory and his throne, as soon as that is accomplished, Satan's place is found no more in heaven (v. 8). There is no case to answer, it is 'open and shut'. Satan's accusations fall flat (Romans 8:33, 34) and he is cast out of heaven into the earth (v. 9).

John hears a loud voice rejoicing in the accomplishment of salvation and the downfall of Satan (v. 10). Believer, this is what we stand in the good of. Satan is mortally defeated. What accomplishes the triumph is the blood of the Lamb (v. 11), and the faith of the saints and their testimony. Just think of the theme of triumph in Hebrews 11. The writer lists Old Testament saint after Old Testament saint, every one of them accused by Satan but every one of them vindicated by faith in Christ's blood which redeemed them, too.

Where does that leave us? In verse 12 we see rejoicing in heaven; salvation is accomplished and eternal safety and bliss is secured for the redeemed who have gone there. But we also see a pronouncement of woe upon the earth because Satan is banished there in all his fury, knowing his doom is certain and his time is limited. The picture is somewhat like Hitler from June 1944 to May 1945. He refused to surrender in the face of certain defeat and in the process inflicted eleven more months of futile death and destruction.

Earthly Persecution

In verse 13 we see that the direct result of Satan's earthly banishment is persecution for the woman who (v. 6) is in 'wilderness separation' from the world. Again, we aim to look at this in more detail later, but for now, understand this. The battle for supremacy and unchallenged sovereignty over God's creation is won. It is just a matter of time, or shall we say 3½ times? Winston Churchill knew when the might and wealth of the USA came in on the side of the United Kingdom in WWII, Hitler's defeat was writ large. The path ahead for the church in the face of Satan's opposition might be 'blood, toil, tears and sweat' but the final outcome is certain victory. Therefore rejoice! (v. 12).

Chapter 15

A Defeated, Vengeful Dragon

Revelation 12:13-17

Chapters 12 to 14 of Revelation provide the fourth of the seven visions of the whole book. It is a vision of creation history from the perspective of the conflict that exists between Satan and God's people, who 'keep the commandments of God and have the testimony of Jesus Christ' (v. 17)[13]. The church of God, as distinct from wider Christendom, may seem irrelevant on the world's stage, but Satan is morbidly obsessed with it, like a cat watching a mouse.

In Revelation 12:1-6 we saw the Old Testament church, the woman with child preparing to bring forth Christ into the world. He is the promised Seed of Genesis 3:15, and he is destined to crush Satan's head by redeeming his church from its sin. Satan's purpose, aware as he was of the promise of the Seed, was to prevent the Seed from coming or destroy him as soon as he did come. Why? Because Satan's objective is his own unchallenged sovereign rule over the created order. In his plan is no place for peace with God through the satisfaction of divine justice. He will spoil God's design by whatever means he can. What is God's plan? Nothing less than the justification of his elect people, his church and Christ's bride, to fit them for his eternal kingdom. Throughout the Old Testament 'half' of created history from the Fall in Eden to the coming of Christ, Satan strove to oppress the woman, the church of true believers in Israel, and then to devour the child when it is born.

But then we are given a different perspective in verses 7 to 12. In heaven, that is, in the realm of spirits, there is war between Satan and his angels on the one side and Michael and his angels on the other side. Satan's angels are the third of God's angels he took with him in rebellion against God (v. 4). This is a war fought with ideas (2 Corinthians 10:4)

---

[13] How do they 'keep the commandments'? Not by legalism but by believing in Christ (John 6:29)

and the issue of contention is whether the Old Testament saints of God in heaven are qualified to be there. As far as Satan is concerned, God has violated his own justice in letting them as sinners enter and remain there. Therefore he, Satan, is called the 'accuser of the brethren' (v. 10). Michael argues that Christ is the 'Lamb slain from the foundation of the world (Revelation 13:8) and his death and shed blood pays the price of redemption for these Old Testament saints, and qualifies them for glory. But Satan insists that as Christ's death has not yet happened, as far as time is concerned, their presence in heaven is unjustifiable. However, as soon as Christ died in time and rose from the dead and ascended into heaven, Satan's argument is undeniably defeated (v. 8).

The Defeat Of Satan
Satan had argued that the Old Testament saints were his because they were sinners and not justified to be in heaven. Michael, the chief of God's angels rebutted his argument by insisting Christ, the promised Seed of the woman (Genesis 3:15) was the Lamb slain from the foundation of the world. Satan insisted propitiation must be seen in time to be of justifying worth and he kept on accusing (v. 10). Then Christ came (v. 5), made of a woman (Galatians 4:4) and, despite Satan watching the woman, he did not know exactly where Christ would be born. Does this not show how limited is his power, his knowledge and his presence? Satan employs Herod to try to get the Magi to reveal the whereabouts of the child, despite the star being visible but again he is thwarted (Matthew 2:12). Joseph, Mary and the infant child flee to Egypt and Christ escapes the murder of the young male children vindictively ordered by Herod.

Jesus grows into a man in relative obscurity apart from a recorded exchange with the elders in the temple at Jerusalem when he was twelve years old. He reaches about 30 years of age and embarks upon his public ministry. Right at its start he, as God incarnate, the Suffering Servant, is subjected to Satan's temptation in the wilderness[14]. I am sure this temptation is because God said to Satan, as he did concerning Job, "have you considered my servant, Jesus?" God's purpose being to prove the Son of Man sinless, and therefore a fitting Passover sacrifice for his people. Throughout the ministry of Jesus, Satan seeks constantly to have him destroyed by the Pharisees and the Romans but, as Jesus frequently says, his hour is not yet come. Nevertheless, he spends much of his time in Galilee outside of Judea until the fourth Passover of his ministry. Then

---

[14] By this wilderness, we mean a literal place away from the hustle and bustle of human society.

he went to Jerusalem for his hour had now come. Satan entered into Judas Iscariot (Luke 22:3) and he could see his prey, Christ, the promised Seed, in his clutches at last.

Think of Satan's delight; the Seed is going to be destroyed; God's plan is in process of failing monumentally! Christ is nailed to the cross and lifted up to die! What a triumph for Satan! He is dead, buried, his followers scattered. But wait, Christ has risen from the dead. He has fully, perfectly, satisfied divine justice for his elect people! His shed blood, the life being in the blood (Deuteronomy 12:23) has atoned and paid their sin-debt. Redemption is accomplished! Satan accuses in heaven but his arguments have been rendered impotent (Romans 8:33, 34). His weapons of heavenly warfare are useless. He has no more power nor any grounds to claim God's people for his own and so, 'we are more than conquerors through him that loved us' (Romans 8:37). Read again Revelation 12:9-11; and declare with me, "Hallelujah!". God has triumphed, Satan has had his house plundered (Matthew 12:29) and he is a defeated foe of God. Is this the end of him? No, (v. 9) he is cast out of heaven into the earth and it is woe to the earth and its inhabitants because an angry devil is cast down into the earth (v. 12).

The Place For The Woman
The furious dragon, thwarted in his purposes to destroy the Christ of God, is cast into the earth and, we read in verse 13, there he persecuted the woman which brought forth the man child. Why does he persecute her? Is his cause not completely lost? Yes, but he persecutes in an attempt to prevent more children being born in her, more sinners being converted to Christ under the preaching of the gospel. But even in this, he is not able to hinder God's purpose. Not one of the sinners chosen in Christ before the foundation of the world shall ever be lost. All shall arrive safe in glory at the end. But let us now think of the situation for the woman after the man child has been victorious over Satan.

In verse 6, immediately after Christ ascended, the woman fled into the wilderness. God had prepared a place for her in the wilderness and there she will be fed for 1,260 days. Verse 14 also tells us the woman is given two great wings of an eagle so she might fly to the wilderness, to her prepared place, where she is nourished in a situation beyond reach of the serpent (v. 9) who is Satan. In verse 14, the duration of her stay is given as a time, times and half a time.

First, what is the wilderness spoken of here? It certainly is not a literal wilderness of desert and scrub. I suspect most believers reading this

107

would declare they live in the midst of human civilisation with all of the modern conveniences of comfortable homes and services. A literal wilderness is not what is meant. No, this wilderness is the 'non-worldliness' of the church, the set-apartness of God's people. It signifies their spiritual ethos, the things of God in which they delight, the service of God and eternal glory to which they aspire. It refers to the things true believers love, and the things they hate. Certainly, individual believers are called upon to strive to live at peace with all men, to be kind, generous-spirited, friendly and sociable so far as possible without violating the principles of God's commandments (v. 17). But the true church is as much a part of the world as the Sahara Desert is integrated with London's West End. Individual believers have to live in the world but we are not of the world. This is why it is futile to try to mingle the church and the politics of the world, even though individual believers may be politicians and work in government to earn a living.

To understand what I mean by this wilderness separation from the world, think back to how you lived before you believed the gospel. You 'walked according to the course of this world' (Ephesians 2:2). You had your conversation there and you fulfilled the desires of your mind and the lusts of your flesh. You had no thought for the service of God. You were indeed, 'children of wrath even as others'. Then, things changed when you believed the gospel, learned the fear of God, repented of your sin, and trusted Christ. This was because you had been quickened by the Holy Spirit. A new man had been born in you. Your desires are now toward the things of God and his people. Is it not so? Those things of the world you used to delight in, you now increasingly find unpleasant. You find the conversation of the ungodly grates upon your new sensitivity to what is pure and wholesome (Philippians 4:8). Though the flesh fights with the spirit and vice versa until we put off this robe of sinful flesh, nevertheless, this is God putting you, as a believer, as a church member, in the wilderness place prepared for his people. This is not to make you feel superior to your fellow men and women still happy in the world. No, the reason God has provided a wilderness place for his church in this world is because Satan is not able to survive or operate there. He can operate effectively only in the world of sin opposed to the rule of God.

How does the woman get to the wilderness away from Satan's clutches? Verse 14 tells us she is given two great wings of an eagle. God's word often speaks of eagles' wings. In Exodus 19:4 we read, 'Ye have seen what I did unto the Egyptians, and how I bare you on eagles' wings, and brought you unto myself.' These eagles' wings are a very effective means of escape, but what do they picture?

I believe these are wings of faith. 1 John 5:4, 5 says, 'For whatsoever is born of God overcometh the world: and this is the victory that overcometh the world, even our faith. Who is he that overcometh the world, but he that believeth that Jesus is the Son of God?' It is by faith that believers escape the world where Satan has them in his clutches (Ephesians 2:8). Faith is the means of flight to God's wilderness of non-worldliness, the place prepared for his church in this world. Faith is sight of the soul given by God. Man does not have faith naturally, irrespective of intelligence or education. It is upon the wings of faith that believers are able to live in the world yet not be of it. As long as they are in that wilderness Satan is unable to reach them (v. 14). I feel sure this is why John is keen to stress in his epistles the need for separation from the world and exhorts believers not to love the world.

Provided and protected as this wilderness is, it is not a comfortable eternal existence, particularly given the weakness of the flesh and the continued presence of a furious, vindictive, Satan in the world. Therefore, we are assured it is for but a limited time, 1,260 days or, once again, time, times and half a time. This is the symbolical 3½ years, 'half' of creation's total duration. It is a long time but a limited time, the time from Christ's ascension until his final return in judgment.

Satan's Flood

We know from verse 12 Satan has 'great wrath' because of his failure to stop Christ Jesus achieving his purposes in coming to save his people from their sins. He knows he is finished and he is furiously vindictive like Hitler when it became clear the Allies would surely win WWII in a matter of time. Hitler continued to grasp at mad notions of victory right to the end despite the needless death and destruction his schemes inflicted. So it is with Satan. He knows his time is limited (v. 12).

In his fury he focuses on the woman (vv. 13, 17) but he cannot get to her so long as she is in her God-given wilderness. He tries to get her out of the wilderness by sending a flood out of his mouth to sweep the woman away. This is not a flood aimed at drowning the woman. Rather it is a flood to sweep her off her feet, which are fixed on the Rock Christ Jesus, and carry her back into conformity with the world. It is a flood of doctrinal compromise, loss of gospel distinctiveness, and temptation to break God's commandments (v. 17). She is enticed to violate God's gospel precepts, and dilute the testimony of Jesus Christ. Many churches that once stood solidly for the truth of the gospel have lost their footing and been swept along in Satan's flood of ecumenism, antinomianism, legalism and liberalism. All of these are aspects of compromise with the world and false religion.

If we are a true church of God we must be on guard for this flood. We must have the anchor of our souls attached firmly to the Rock. We must confess Jesus Christ to be the promised Messiah of God who fulfilled every decree of God concerning the salvation of his elect. We must testify of his truth and seek always to live for him. Satan is furious with us and with all churches and believers like us. How does he seek to harm us? By having us conform to the world and tempting us to renounce the object of our faith.

Fear Not Little Flock
Jesus told us not to fear even though we are but a little flock, 'it is your Father's good pleasure to give you the kingdom' (Luke 12:32). He tells us in the world we shall suffer trouble but to be of good cheer because he has overcome the world and the Satan of the world (John 16:33). No doubt the path through life for believers is narrow and difficult. We must pass through the valley of the shadow of death and Satan prowls around seeking whom he may devour (1 Peter 5:8). Nevertheless, God has equipped his people with armour, gospel armour, with which to resist and withstand (Ephesians 6:10-20). Believer, do not fear Satan even though we know his objectives. He is not able to pluck you from the Father's hand, he is not strong enough. Take the armour and use it, look to Christ, and comfort and encourage one another.

Chapter 16

The Dragon's War With The Woman's Seed

Revelation 13

In the beginning God created all things perfect and put creation under the rule of the first Adam, but Adam surrendered his God-given kingdom to Satan and subjugated his entire race to Satan's rule. All sin and rebellion against God is intolerable to the nature and law of God. It deserves his just punishment and eternal condemnation. But God has sworn he will have an unrivalled kingdom of righteousness and peace and all rebellion in this creation will be subdued and eternally defeated. God's kingdom will be populated by redeemed rebels, sinners made righteousness through Christ, who as God's Lamb was sacrificed for them (2 Corinthians 5:21). The blood Christ shed has cleansed his people from all their sin. God's purpose shall not fail (Isaiah 42:4).

This world continues and the conflict between God and Satan goes on until the decreed end when a symbolical 1,260 days are accomplished, and the 'time, times and half a time' are completed. In Revelation 12 we saw Satan opposing the woman's seed, that is, opposing members of the church of Christ in this world. We saw him continuing to accuse Old Testament saints in heaven despite Michael's insistence they were justified from all sin by the Lamb slain from the foundation of the world (Revelation 13:8). We saw Satan defeated at Calvary at the moment he was most confident of final victory, and we have seen him cast out into the earth where furious with his hopeless situation, he makes war with the woman and persecutes the church of Christ in this world. God has put the church into a wilderness separation from the world of Satan so he is not able to touch her there. In his fury Satan sends out a flood in an attempt to sweep her off her rock, which is Christ, and into conformity with Satan's world.

But what strategy, what tactics, does Satan use in his enmity against Christ's people? Revelation 13 tells us. In graphic, alarming language we are able to see, in visionary symbol, what Satan is doing today and also what are the limits of his reach.

111

Two Beasts
Revelation 13 gives greater detail about the way Satan makes war with the woman and how he persecutes the church in the world (Revelation 12:13, 17). It is a vision and the images are symbolical not literal, yet they are clear enough. God has given us this vision (Revelation 1:1) so we may recognise Satan's harassment when it happens and so we are not surprised or alarmed by it arising. Hereby we prepare our minds and arm ourselves as saints to stand firm in the darkest hour.

John stands on a sandy beach by the sea where he sees a grotesque beast come out of the water. Then he sees another beast come out of the earth, somewhat less grotesque in appearance, but still speaking as a dragon. What do these visions represent?

The First Beast
We see this beast in verses 1 to 9. It arises out of the sea, that is, not literally the sea but what the sea symbolises. Isaiah 57:20 says, 'But the wicked are like the troubled sea, when it cannot rest, whose waters cast up mire and dirt.' Compare this with Revelation 17:15, 'And he saith unto me, The waters which thou sawest, where the whore sitteth, are peoples, and multitudes, and nations, and tongues.' This sea symbolises the peoples, the nations of the world, humanity in its political and economic striving. Out of this sea of humanity arises a beast with the characteristics of Satan, the Dragon of Revelation (12:9). The beast has seven heads, ten horns and ten crowns and speaks blasphemy against God (v. 6). He has the combined appearance of a leopard, a lion and a bear, features which link this vision with Daniel's in Daniel 7:2-6. These beasts speak of earthly kingdoms and political powers, but the beast in Revelation 13:1 is a combination, a unification of opposing world powers all deriving power from Satan, the dragon.

In verse 3 we read an odd fact about this monster; one of its heads had been mortally wounded but here it is healed and all the world is enthralled with the beast's appearance. If this beast represents unified world power, as I believe it does, what could the healed wound refer to? In Genesis 10 and 11, following the flood when the world was once more significantly populated with people, the sin of Adam's race was again rampant. A strong leader, Nimrod, had arisen. His name is more like 'rebellious panther' than the description 'mighty hunter' of the KJV Bible. The peoples of the then world were unified in language and purpose and they came together at Babel, which became Babylon, and set about building a tower to reach to heaven. Whatever that amounted to in reality, it most certainly represented man's rebellion against the rule and justice of God and it sought to reach heaven without the satisfaction of divine justice promised in the Messiah.

God 'wounded' this one nation by confounding the people's speech into mutually incomprehensible languages. This began the existence of separate nation states and with it, Babel's political unity was divided. Now, in the vision of Revelation 13:3, the wound is healed and barriers between nations are being removed. There is a desire among the world's political leaders to open borders, establish international norms and rule by such organisations as the United Nations. They want to encourage trading blocs like the European Union, and generally dismantle national distinctions for a wider 'brotherhood of man' and political union. The wound is also healed by translation skills that greatly diminish the problem of language separation. I have an app on my smartphone that can listen to foreign languages and turn them in real time into English, and vice versa. Keep in mind this union of humanity is inherently antagonistic to the gospel. It is opposed to the necessity of blood redemption for the righteousness required by the justice of God.

We read that all the world wondered after the beast and all gave willing allegiance to the beast, despite the utterances of his mouth. He was speaking great things and blasphemies against the name of God, against his tabernacle and against the heavenly host. These are blasphemies of denial of God's truth, denial of God's sovereignty and contempt for gospel redemption symbolised by the tabernacle in verse 6.

Looking back over long centuries of history, it would be very difficult to align political events of the past with the vision of this first beast, but the changes of the last 200 years, and especially the last 30 years, make it easy to see its manifestation in today's world politics. It might not have come to full fruition yet, but the signs are clear and growing. Now let us look at the second beast.

The Second Beast
From the same vantage point, John sees a second beast (v. 11). This time it comes up from the earth. The earth is more stable than the sea and we can take this to indicate a distinction from the political and economic instability of the nations as they strive for unity. This is something that goes on independent of the first beast's political manifestation.

The first beast was monstrous and grotesque yet mesmerising to humanity. This second beast seems at first glance like Christ. It has the appearance of a lamb, but this lamb has horns of power and it speaks like a dragon, with the voice of Satan. It also is in league with the first beast and encourages the worship of the first beast. What marks it out from the first beast is that it does 'great wonders'. I take it these wonders are those of science and technology, philosophy and religion. They have been on parade especially in the last 200 years from the Industrial Revolution, but peaked in the last 30 years or so with the rise of the open internet. Now one new thing comes hot on the heels of another. People are seduced by these wonders. They are key to prosperity in material things. They encompass godless, evolutionary thinking. They champion the supremacy of rationality[15], and exploit international travel, instant worldwide communications and all forms of modern, technological wizardry.

So enthralling and attractive to mankind is the allure of the second beast that he deceives them with his miracles. He tells them to make an image of the first beast, to give themselves an object, as it were, for their worship. It is not the first time political leaders have set up images and forced everyone to bow down. The Chaldean empire, Babylon, under its emperor Nebuchadnezzar, was an attempt by Satan to achieve worldwide political unity by force while denying the true God. Nebuchadnezzar set up an image to be worshipped (Daniel 3) and Daniel, God's prophet, was sentenced to death by lion for refusing to bow down and conform. Daniel would certainly have died had not God stopped the mouths of the beasts. These Revelation 13 beasts are brutally unforgiving of dissenters as any believer who questions the accepted morals and practices of our day will quickly discover. The 'killing' of verse 15 might be in the form of ridicule or ostracising, or in some cultures even violence and death. Verse 16 tells us it is not just isolated incidents of persecution for dissenters but a general restriction on their ability to do business, trade and operate in human society. We have seen little of these things as yet, but for true Christians there are tell-tale signs of their approach. For example, there are subjects they can no longer study at university because of the aggressive rationalism that denies the Christian God. As I said before, although I have a record as an effective physics and general science teacher from the 1970s, I doubt I would be offered a job today or be able, if I was, to teach aspects of the syllabus because of its alignment with the image of the beast.

We still have not identified these beasts clearly. They are not Satan but all of their power is derived from him. In Revelation 19:20 the second

---

[15] A key tenet of modern 'scientific' thinking is the supremacy of rationality. It is claimed that everything is explainable by purely physical laws and the one notion that is forbidden is any acknowledgement of the possibility of Intelligent Design, i.e. the workings of God.

beast is identified as the 'false prophet' and it is clear from later chapters of Revelation that together the first and second beasts constitute Antichrist. Antichrist is everything that is against Christ and opposed to the gospel of his grace. It is manifested in the world where nations seek ever closer political unity and seen in mesmerising technology and hypnotic amusements by which millions are seduced.[16] The beasts put their mark on people, just as God seals his own in their foreheads (Revelation 7:3). Everybody has one mark or the other but never both, for, said Jesus, you cannot serve God and mammon. Those without the beast's mark are unable to trade.

In the last verse of the chapter we read of the number of the beast. It is the same as the number of man (v. 18). It is 666. A lot of superstitious, silly nonsense has been written about this symbol. The A666 road runs from Bolton to Manchester in the north of England and some gullible people are frightened to drive along it. What is the significance of 666? It is six times ten squared plus six times ten plus six. Six is the number of man because it falls one short of seven, the number of God. Six is the number of days of creation, one short of the seventh day in which God is to be worshipped and honoured. The number 666 speaks of the fulness of man in creation without God; the kingdom of this world without God. The beasts of Antichrist signify the highest development of man's sovereignty over creation, yet without God and under the thrall of Satan.

But again we are assured the duration of the influence of Antichrist is limited. In verse 5 we read of power given to him to continue forty and two months. We have seen this number before and noted it is the same duration as 1,260 days, the time, times and half a time, or 3½ years of the woman's sojourn in God's wilderness place. Why is it presented as 42? It is six, the number of the beast and the number of man, working on seven, the perfection of God. Man striving to achieve divine perfection yet always failing.

Christ And Antichrist
Throughout the period from the Fall in Eden to the return of Christ at the end of time there is conflict between God and Satan. God has Christ to glorify his person and save his people. Satan has Antichrist to blaspheme God, enthral mankind and to deceive men with lying signs and wonders.

---

[16] I am not saying that technology *per se* is bad; we all make use of it and none more importantly than true churches using it to broadcast the gospel. But it displays Antichrist when swathes of people are utterly seduced by it, enthralled to it, and blinded to the truth of God.

Read 2 Thessalonians 2:3-12 for yourself and see also John's epistles, for example, 1 John 2:18, 22; 4:3; 2 John 7. There is plenty of scriptural warning corroborating the reality of Antichrist. Antichrist is always present throughout the 42 months but it is not yet revealed at the peak of its manifestation. Nevertheless, the seeds are sprouting and growing fast. I do not know exactly how it will ultimately be manifested but there is a clear indication of times becoming very difficult for God's true people, possibly more difficult than ever before.

The Outworking Of The Vision
We are not able to stop the beasts coming to the fulness of Antichrist, nor can we halt the world's wholesale worship of the image of the beast. It is useless to seek refuge in national politics or by signing petitions and voting for parties if our purpose is to stop the revealed word of God from coming to fruition[17]. We submit to the powers that be, certainly, but God's people will not worship the image of the beast (v. 8). They are sealed with God's seal (Revelation 7:3) not with the beast's mark (v. 16). God's election of his people guarantees their faithfulness (Romans 8:28-32).

If you are God's child you will have an ear with which to hear God's voice speaking (v. 9). And although Satan and his Antichrist can subtly appear as an 'angel of light' (2 Corinthians 11:14), able to deceive even the elect if that were possible, be assured it is not possible. You will have God-given discernment sufficient for the day. Verse 10 speaks of the 'patience and faith of the saints'. This enables them to endure hardship confident that God will keep them and take them safe to glory. It also gives them confidence that those terrible oppressors of God's people who take captive and kill, will themselves be taken captive and 'killed'.

Finally, in verse 18, if you have the 'wisdom of God', that is, the wisdom which 'Christ is made unto us' (1 Corinthians 1:30, Colossians 2:3), you will see the fatal shortfall of 666, of man without God and of Satan's subjects without Christ. Antichrist has but a short time anyway (Revelation 12:12) and for the elect's sake the days of trouble will be further shortened (Matthew 24:22). Brothers and sisters in Christ, do not be afraid, the God who has revealed these things to us is the same God who rules over them. We may experience great difficulties in this life on

---

[17] I am not calling for a boycott on voting in elections. It is a believer's duty to be a good citizen and respect political authority. Yet we should not think that by voting we can change the direction of what God has permitted Satan to do and accomplish before his final destruction.

earth but God will keep us throughout and take us to be with him. For now, take the armour provided (Ephesians 6:10-20) and stand fast, but also, take a peek forward to Revelation 14:1. There you will see Christ and his people on this earth. Rather than squirming under tyrannical oppression, as the heathen rage and imagine a vain thing against the Lord and his anointed (Psalm 2), rejoice! He that dwells in the heavens laughs them to scorn.

Chapter 17

Eternal Blessedness Or Eternal Torment?

Revelation 14:1-12

Revelation 14 brings us to the end of the fourth vision of the seven visions of the entire book. The whole of the fourth vision, from its start in chapter 12, has revealed to us the spiritual warfare going on throughout the time of this creation. Spiritual warfare between God and Satan and their respective kingdoms. We have seen profound impacts on the people of God in this world, but at the same time, we have seen good reason to remain patient and confident of the final state of bliss in heaven. Chapter 14 reinforces this view.

Throughout the book of Revelation we have observed a sequence of great contrasts. For example, in chapter 6 we saw six seals opened with dramatic effects on this world and its peoples. In chapter 7, by contrast, we saw 144,000 people sealed with God's glorious salvation. In chapter 9 we saw two dreadful woes. Then, in chapter 10 we saw a vision of the Mighty Angel, our Lord Jesus Christ with his little book showing us he remains in supreme control whatever the seals, trumpets and woes bring to the earth. In chapter 13 we saw the fearful vision of the two beasts of Satan, his Antichrist, of which we shall see more later. The chapter ended with a chilling warning of believers finding themselves increasingly at odds with Satan's kingdom to the extent they will find it virtually impossible to trade or interact with the world in an economic sense. Then, immediately, chapter 14 shows us the victorious kingdom of Christ. Chapter 13 contrasts chapter 14, with the dark vision of the beast and his kingdom highlighting the bright vision of the Lamb and his redeemed people. If we consider these adjacent chapters as contrary perspectives rather than a sequence of events, we see in chapter 13 the triumphant perspective of Antichrist, and in chapter 14 the triumphant perspective of Christ.

The Will Of The Father

In what is called 'The Lord's Prayer' in Matthew 6, Jesus taught his disciples to pray, 'Thy will be done'. What is the will of our Father in heaven? It is that Christ be given the kingdom; that the whole creation should be subject to his rule and all rebellion and opposition be put down and defeated. In the kingdom of Christ will be all the people of the Father's choice, God's elect. They are all purified from sin having been washed and redeemed by the blood of God's Son, so that our Lord can say, "This is the will of my Father, that of all that he has given me I should lose nothing" (John 6:39). He performed his Father's will perfectly, being obedient even to the death of the cross. As a man he prayed for the cup of suffering be taken from him, but willingly condescended to drink it to its dregs. "Not my will but thine be done".

This is a complete contrast to the will of Satan for his kingdom. His is a kingdom of lies, of godlessness, sin, selfishness, hatred, cruelty and deceit. But, above all, it is a kingdom with no blood redemption and no satisfaction for God's justice. I ask you, do you believe this? Do you see there are only two camps and you are either in the one or the other? You cannot 'sit on the fence' about this.

Two Perspectives

I must stress and underline this. Chapter 13 shows us the perspective of Antichrist. It portrays the worldwide supremacy of the kingdom of darkness and the willing submission and support of the majority of the world's peoples. We see them stamped with the mark of the beast and thus enabled to 'trade' and do the business of natural life while the people sealed with God's seal of conversion (Revelation 7:3), and without the beast's mark, are excluded from buying and selling. These days are so bad they are to be shortened for the elect's sake (Mark 13:20).

We saw another perspective on this in chapter 11. There God's two witnesses, his church and his preachers, lay dead in the street of the world. It was a dreadful, seemingly hopeless vision and we already see in these days the widespread reality of it with the true church, at least in the eyes of the world and false religion, as good as dead. But how things appear is not always as they really are. Remember Elisha in 2 Kings 6:15? He was surrounded by the forces of Assyria while Israel, symbolical of the people of God, were in utter disarray. Elisha's young servant laments that their case is hopeless but Elisha prays to God to open his eyes to see the spiritual reality of the situation. Then what did he see? A host of angels on their side, completely outnumbering the Assyrian army. That is what we have in Revelation 14.

Having seen in vision such dreadful things at the end of chapter 13, John now looks and sees a Lamb on Mount Sion (Zion). With him stands a great throng, 144,000 marked in their foreheads with the Father's name. John is seeing with the eye of faith what the natural man cannot receive or know (1 Corinthians 2:14). He has been lifted up on wings of faith to see the spiritual warfare from the perspective of the kingdom of Christ. All the while the dreadful kingdom of Antichrist is working out its evil purpose in the earth, the redeemed of Christ, his 144,000 present in the world at the same time, are simultaneously with Christ on Mount Zion. Mount Zion is where Jehovah dwells symbolically among his people on earth, pictured by physical Jerusalem in the Old Testament, but realised as the church of Christ throughout the world in New Testament times. The Lamb with his 144,000 on Mount Zion is the church of true believers in this world; it is God's stronghold of supreme power all the while that Satan's kingdom of Antichrist seems to prosper.

Psalm 2

We have referred to Psalm 2 in earlier chapters. At this point in Revelation it again provides an instructive perspective. All around us the kingdom of Satan rages, the world's 'nations' as the Psalmist puts it. They imagine a vain thing against the Lord and his Anointed. They seek to cast off all of the restraint of God's holiness and justice because they feel they are 'bands and cords' tying them up and preventing them from living exactly as they want to. But God laughs at the futility of their scheming.

What does this tell us? Whatever the world, the kingdom of Antichrist, tries to do to the kingdom of Christ and its people in the world, be it making war, persecuting, or making life as difficult as they can, Christ's people are still here! Not one of them is ever lost. They are living stones in the temple of God (1 Peter 2:5). Each one cut from the quarry of humanity and fitted exactly into its place. They are dry bones brought to life, soldiers in the ranks of God's army that Ezekiel saw (Ezekiel 37:10).

In the kingdom of Satan and his Antichrist, the 144,000 suffer because they refuse to worship the beast (Revelation 13:8) and because their names are written in the Lamb's book of life. It may be in this world they are 'killed all the day long and accounted as sheep for the slaughter' (Romans 8:36), but they alone have spiritual, eternal life.

Read the rest of Psalm 2; look at the supremacy of the kingdom of God; look at God's King, the Lord Jesus Christ, see him set upon his holy hill of Zion. God has sworn that Christ will triumph. Whose camp are

121

you in? Are you still in the camp of the kingdom of Antichrist? You need to be wise and learn from God. 'Kiss the Son lest he be angry and ye perish from the way when his wrath is kindled but a little' (Psalm 2:12).

The Song Of The Redeemed
In verses 2 and 3, John heard a voice from heaven, a very loud voice, with music and singing. It is the song of all the 144,000s ever to have lived on earth and now in glory. It is the song of the 'redeemed', those bought with a price, paid for with the only currency of real value, the precious blood of the Lamb. We saw them in Revelation 5:9, in the second vision, singing this song, 'and they sung a new song, saying, Thou art worthy to take the book, and to open the seals thereof: for thou wast slain, and hast redeemed us to God by thy blood out of every kindred and tongue and people and nation.'

These are people like everyone else, sinners by nature and by action, each one owing a huge debt to the law and justice of God. As such they are captives of Satan and his kingdom of Antichrist. But Christ the God-man has come in flesh, and having been made the sin of these people, has paid its debt to the law by his death at Calvary. The law requires death for sin. The soul that sins shall die (Ezekiel 18:4). This is the 'curse of the law', but Christ redeemed his people from the curse of the law by being made a curse for them (Galatians 3:13). Now God's justice is perfectly satisfied and God has justified those who are by nature sinners (Romans 3:26). He is a 'just God and a Saviour' (Isaiah 45:21). Why is it these people and not everybody that ever lived? Because these are the elect of God, chosen in Christ before the foundation of the world, loved with God's everlasting love. They have been sealed in their foreheads (Revelation 7:3), brought out of servitude to Satan, given spiritual life and discernment (1 Corinthians 2:14) and set on the 'narrow way' to eternal glory from the 'broad way' that leads to destruction and hell.

Virgins
In verse 4, the redeemed are described as virgins who are not defiled with women. This is not talking about supposedly celibate priests or any such nonsense. It is about spiritual adultery, fornication and impurity. Often Old Testament Israel, the symbolical people of God, is pictured as an adulterous woman on account of idolatry and compromise with false religion. But the Israel of God (Galatians 6:16) has steadfastly refused to be compromised with religious fornication. God's true Israel is kept by the Holy Spirit, kept true and faithful to Christ and his doctrine. They have been given the 'mind of Christ' and as a result, the Psalmist tells us

in Psalm 119:99, 'I have more understanding than all my teachers for thy testimonies are my meditation.' As it says in Revelation 14:4, they follow the Lamb wherever he leads them because Jesus said, 'my sheep hear my voice, and I know them, and they follow me' (John 10:27).

God's true Israel are further marked out by a purity and holiness not their own by nature but theirs by union with Christ. Christ having been made their sin and paying its debt to the law has resulted in their being made the righteousness of God in him (2 Corinthians 5:21). What more righteousness could they possibly need than God's own righteousness to come before God and be accepted in his sight?

However, while Antichrist seems to grow ever worse and earthly life for God's saints seems set to become ever more difficult, Revelation 14 gives us the Lamb's perspective on his 144,000. He is triumphant. Our God is serenely ruling all things. He laughs at the futile aspirations of Antichrist. Psalm 73 is instructive here, Asaph was 'envious at the wicked' until he went into the sanctuary, representing the gospel. Meditating upon the sanctuary and Christ our peace he sees things from God's perspective. He sees how things will turn out for all who reject God's rightful rule. Are you feeling downcast, believer? Come into the sanctuary of the gospel of God's sovereign grace and particular redemption. There you will see the end of the Satan's kingdom.

Three Angels
In Revelation 14:6-12, John sees a vision of the downfall of Satan's kingdom. Again, this provides a stark contrast to chapter 13 where Satan's kingdom appears so unassailable. Satan's kingdom stands like Goliath defying insignificant David but in verses 6 to 12 the giant's head is severed with minimal ceremony. Three angels, messengers of God, speak God's word, and being God's word, it is as good as done as soon as it is spoken.

The first angel flies in the midst of heaven having the everlasting gospel to preach to them that dwell on the earth, all of them. Is this a 'last chance gospel' to everyone without exception? Is it the 'free offer' so dear to so many who profess faithfulness to Christ? The trouble with presenting the gospel as an offer, free or otherwise, is it supposes an ability in sinners they simply do not have, the ability to exercise their fallen wills to believe the gospel. Natural man is dead in trespasses and sins. The things of God are foolishness to him neither can he know them. God does not send out his angel in the hope that perhaps some in Satan's kingdom will 'open the door to him' this is the error of freewill Arminianism, it is not the doctrine of Christ. The free offer is not the gospel preached by the apostles. They declared the gospel truth that 'Salvation is of the Lord' (Jonah 2:9) and left it to God the Holy Spirit to open men's hearts (Acts 16:14). They were content to know that as many as were ordained to eternal life would believe (Acts 13:48). As Jesus taught his disciples, 'if they will not believe Moses and the prophets, they will not believe even if someone rises from the dead'. The grace of God the Holy Spirit cannot be resisted.

The word gospel means good news. In what respect, then, is this angel's gospel 'good news'? Look at what he actually says with his loud voice (v. 7). He declares, 'fear God and give glory to him'. It is an announcement of the final judgment, the end of all things. It is only good news to God's persecuted people whose 'blood cries out for vengeance' (Revelation 6:10). Yet, he announces it to everyone. Read the following scriptures: Isaiah 45:23-25; Romans 14:11; Philippians 2:8-11. The angel preaching this everlasting gospel is what those scriptures describe. It is the moment when 'every knee shall bow to Christ'.

Then, in verse 8, a second angel announces the fall of Babylon. We shall see clearly in later chapters the full significance of Babylon but for now, suffice to say it represents all false religion. It has its roots in Genesis 10 and 11 with Nimrod, that rebellious panther, his tower of Babel and its aspiration to reach heaven without the satisfaction of divine justice by the blood of Christ. Babylon was the place of captivity for Judah many years later. It represents everything that spiritually seduces men and women away from the service of God, whatever it might be called. But, for now, praise God, it is enough to let God's saints know for sure that the end of Babylon is certain.

In verses 9-11 we have the record of the third angel's pronouncement of hell for all who worship the beast and his image. This encompasses everyone except those whose names are written in the Lamb's book of life (Revelation 13:8). What is hell? I do not know precisely, but I do know on the strength of this angel's testimony it is the withdrawal of all God's temporal, physical blessings on mankind, coupled with the shocking realisation that the promised blessings of Satan's kingdom are a terrible illusion. This realisation and the withdrawal of God's temporal blessings, for time is no more, must by definition, be an unending torment. There is no purgatory, no parole, simply the certainty of hell outside of Christ. Today is the day of salvation. Seek and ye shall find!

Verse 12 provides the conclusion of the matter; wait patiently child of God. Keep looking, in faith, for eternal realities, in certain and sure knowledge that God has saved you out of this fallen world with its Babylonian religion and Satanic oppression.

Chapter 18

Harvest Time

Revelation 14:6-20

The book of Revelation reveals to God's saints the triumph of his kingdom, and the defeat of Satan and his kingdom, which he usurped with Adam's willing support at the Fall in Eden. It reveals to us the restoration of God's rule over all created order.

The book comprises seven visions, each covering either the whole of created time or particularly the time from Christ's ascension until his final return in judgment. The seven visions provide different perspectives and increasing detail, especially of the end, as the visions unfold. The first vision in chapters 1 to 3 reveals the living Christ in the midst of his church on earth throughout the time from his ascension to his return; whatever else happens, he is here in the midst of his churches now. The second vision in chapters 4 to 7 reveals the implementation of the first six seals of the seven-sealed book of the plan of God for the restoration of his kingdom. The third vision in chapters 8 to 11 reveals the opening of the seventh seal of the book, which issues in the sounding of seven trumpets the last three of which are woes, until we read in Revelation 11:5 that the kingdoms of the world become the kingdoms of our Lord and of his Christ. The fourth vision in chapters 12 to 14 shows us the conflict between the Antichrist of Satan and the Christ of God throughout created history, Old Testament and New Testament. Each vision closes with a summary of the end of all things, and as the visions progress towards the end of the book, the detail given of the end appears to increase.

The purpose of the visions is to comfort and encourage God's people on earth living through the effects of the opening of the seals and the sounding of the trumpets which we see unfolding more clearly than ever in these days. The encouragement given is that they should wait patiently for the certainty of glory, with full assurance because everything is always under the supreme control of God.

In this chapter, it is my intention to finish looking at the fourth vision in the latter half of chapter 14. Let us summarise what has gone before in the vision. Chapter 12 showed us Satan's defeat by Christ, the disarming of his accusations against the brethren in glory, and his subsequent fury, war and persecution against the church, exacerbated by his knowledge that his time is limited. Chapter 13 than painted a gruesome picture of the vile kingdom of Satan's Antichrist which is this world, its politics, economics, philosophy, science, morality, values and religion. The second beast works signs and wonders with technologies to mesmerise the peoples of the world. Chapter 13 ended with the symbolism in the number 666 showing Satan's certain failure. In chapter 14 we were shown that in spite of the horror of the kingdom of Antichrist, and while the church finds it ever more difficult to conduct necessary trade in the world, it is, in fact, quite safe. God's people are safe in Christ, all the symbolical 144,000 of them, safe on Mount Zion in this world. Chapter 14 ends with the confident assertion the church's troubles do not go on indefinitely. The end of all things is announced and the headline is clear; 'Glory For God's Elect And Hell For Every Rebel'.

Announcement Of The End
We saw in the last chapter in verses 6 to 11 three angels announce the end of all things. The first one effectively issues a call for every knee to bow to Christ. This is good news, the 'everlasting gospel' (v. 6), to the people of God. The second angel pronounces the fall of Babylon which includes all false religion, which is blatantly Christ-less and promises heaven without the satisfaction of God's justice. It includes the majority of Christendom which has made a covenant with death (Isaiah 28:15) whilst thinking it is doing God service (Matthew 7:22). The third angel announces the certain reality of hell. In summary, the end is coming, the writing is on the wall for Satan's kingdom as surely as it was for Belshazzar's kingdom (Daniel 5:25). All rebellion against the rule of God will receive its just and certain reward. But what about God's saints, his church?

The Wheat Harvest
The first vision of Revelation promises eternal blessings to God's people who 'overcome' and remain faithful to Christ in the face of worldly, anti-Christ opposition. The second vision pictures an innumerable multitude of God's people in eternal bliss. The third vision pictures judgment on the nations, that is, upon Satan's kingdom, and reward for God's servants

and prophets. Now, the fourth vision pictures the end as a two-stage harvest, that of the wheat then that of the grapes.

Although the word 'wheat' is not specifically used here, it is clearly implied from elsewhere in scripture. The gathering of God's saints from the earth immediately prior to the final judgment is pictured as the reaping of a great wheat harvest. Those pictured as the wheat in the harvest are 'the saints' (v. 12). This simply means 'set apart ones'. They are set apart from the rest of humanity by God in his sovereign electing grace before the world began. They are chosen in Christ, called in union with him from eternity, and justified in him as the Lamb slain from the foundation of the world (Revelation 13:8). These saints were born sinners like everyone else descended from Adam. They were children of wrath (Ephesians 2:4) and dead in trespasses and sins, but they have been quickened by God the Holy Spirit. Thus quickened, the saints are given eyes to see spiritual truth and faith to believe in Christ. They live by the faith of the Son of God (Galatians 2:21). They rest justified by God in Christ. They establish God's law by faith, living separate from the world. 'For our conversation' or citizenship, says Philippians 3:20, 'is in heaven, from whence also we look for the Saviour, the Lord Jesus Christ.'

In verse 13 a voice from heaven describes the saints as blessed; they are 'blessed from henceforth'. What could that mean? From henceforth means from the announcement of the end of all things. Certainly, all are blessed who die in the Lord. 'Precious in the sight of the Lord is the death of his saints' (Psalm 116:15). Jesus promised the penitent thief on the cross he would be with him in Paradise that very day. But this voice is pronouncing the final blessing when the end of all things is set in motion. This is blessing with all the fulness of eternal glory in the presence of God. The whole elect of God will be together then in glory. There they all will rest from their labours, they will enter into the full appreciation of eternal Sabbath rest in the finished work of Christ. All of their struggles with the kingdom of Antichrist will be at an end for ever.

Then we are told 'their works do follow them'. What works are these? Is this speaking of progressive sanctification by improving law works for which they expect degrees of rewards compared with one another? Not at all! The parable of the vineyard and the labourers teaches the principle that whatever length of service the saints give to the kingdom of God, they all are rewarded equally. Saints' only currency is the finished work of Christ. Rather, the works spoken of here are 'works of faith' (John 6:28, 29) which issue from quiet conformance of life to gospel precepts. Perhaps Matthew 25:31-40 is instructive on this point; the Son of Man commends his true people at the judgment for their works of charity of

127

which seemingly they are unaware. In this way, I believe, the works of the saints follow them. The reprobate in contrast are full of boasting for their service and for what they feel they have done in his name.

In verses 14 to 16 we see the saints taken out of the world immediately before the final judgment, not in any sort of 'secret rapture', but echoing Revelation 11:12, 13. Noah and Lot were respectively taken out of the place of judgment immediately prior to it falling, first in the flood and later in Sodom by fire and brimstone. Note the harvest is taken by Christ himself, the Son of Man. He it is that enters heaven announcing, 'Behold, I and the children whom the Lord hath given me' (Isaiah 8:18). He is the Lord of Hosts (Psalm 24:10) that leads his triumphant host through the everlasting doors of glory. He does it at the time decreed by the Father, when the harvest is ripe, when the 3½ 'times' are finished. Then, what we read in 1 Thessalonians 4:16-18 will come to pass, 'For the Lord himself shall descend from heaven with a shout, with the voice of the archangel, and with the trump of God: and the dead in Christ shall rise first: Then we which are alive and remain shall be caught up together with them in the clouds, to meet the Lord in the air: and so shall we ever be with the Lord. Wherefore comfort one another with these words.'

Will you be among those whom Christ will take out of this world to glory? It depends where your treasure is. Is it in heaven or in this world? Will you be like Lot's wife in the end? Though seemingly taken out of the place of judgment to safety, she looked back, and just like all the neighbours she left behind was turned to a pillar of salt because her heart was fixed firmly in Sodom (see Luke 17:32-37).

The Grape Harvest

With the wheat harvest gathered safely in, we come to verse 17. Another angel comes to gather the clusters of the vine of the earth. These grapes are the peoples of the world who worship the image of the beast, and reject the rule of Christ. These are the multitudes who are not qualified to be taken in the wheat harvest. They have not been justified by Christ's atonement. They are still bearing their own sin and crying out in rebellion against God. In so doing they have willingly placed themselves beyond the reach of his mercy. The preaching of the gospel is no more. The day of grace and salvation is past. They rejected Christ in life, now he leaves them to his angels to reap for judgment. Instead of the eternal rest and glory reserved for the saints, these are cast into the winepress of the wrath of God.

Many people try to speculate, sometimes in vivid detail, about what this could mean. I am neither able nor prepared to do that. Let us aim not to go beyond what God has revealed. Yet, this much is clear, when God's people have been taken out of the way, the final destruction of life on this earth will be unleashed. In recent years we have feared nuclear annihilation arising from the Cold War, today we fear Islamic Jihad, but whether any of this is indicated in these verses the end result is the same. It is a river of blood (v. 20) that is 1600 furlongs long up to the depth of the horse's bridles. Four is the number of the world of people and ten is the number of worldly completeness; $1600 = (4 \times 10)^2$ and I believe this basically means 'all of it'. There is no escape for the ungodly from judgment despite their frantic efforts even to get mountains to fall on them (Revelation 6:16).

Our God is holy and just. He would cease to be God if in any way he failed to honour his own law and justice by letting sinners go free without satisfaction being made to offended justice. He will most certainly repay what his justice demands. Will you heed the clear warning? Will you cry out as did the Philippian jailer, "What must I do to be saved?" The answer today is unchanged from the reply Paul gave all those years ago. "Believe on the Lord Jesus Christ and thou shalt be saved ..."

Chapter 19

Antichrist's Final Defeat

Revelation 15 and 16

Chapters 15 and 16 belong together and form the fifth vision of the seven visions that comprise the whole book of Revelation. The fifth vision provides more of what we have seen in earlier visions, but here we have a new perspective. We see increased detail and intensity in the judgments poured out in the seven vials of chapter 16. This is because the focus is increasingly towards the end of all things. We have read of similar judgments in earlier visions because they are present to varying degrees throughout space-time history, but now we see them intensifying towards the final judgment. Be sure to remember the purpose of the visions. They are to comfort God's believing people, to increase their assurance of eternal bliss and glory, and to encourage patience as we wait for the end to come. Also, do not overlook the warning contained here to unbelievers to flee to Christ for safety from the wrath that is to come.

I intend to deal with this vision quickly in one chapter aiming not to be too shallow whilst avoiding wearying the reader with overmuch repetition; please do not be wearied by it. It is given to show us more of what must shortly come to pass as God gains the final victory over Satan and his kingdom of Antichrist. God is showing us how he is answering the prayer Christ taught his disciples to pray, 'Thy kingdom come. Thy will be done in earth as it is in heaven' (Matthew 6:10).

In this vision seven vials of wrath are poured out upon the earth, God's people are removed and the church is seen in glory.

Seven Vials Poured Out

In earlier visions we saw the seven-sealed book and the Lion of the Tribe of Judah. The Lion is also the Lamb of God, the only one qualified to open the seals which implement God's plan of salvation and triumph over Satan. Six seals were opened, all to some extent frustrating Satan's purpose of worldwide, Christ-less unity. When the seventh seal was opened it revealed seven trumpets of even more intense judgment, the seventh of which (Revelation 11:15) is further unfolded in chapter 16 as seven vials of wrath. The wrath of God speaks of his infinite holiness in contrast to sin. These seven vials spell the final end of Satan's kingdom. He knew when defeated at Calvary he had but a short time (Revelation 12:12) and now this short time has finally run out.

Earlier visions have given us varying perspectives on the same end. In the second vision, in Revelation 6:12, when the sixth seal was opened there was a glimpse of the end with earthquakes, cosmic cataclysm and people fleeing from wrath. In Revelation 11:15 the seventh trumpet sounded and the vision was of lightning, voices, thunderings, earthquake and great hail, all accompanying God's final victory. Then in Revelation 14:17-20 we saw the final harvest of the world, the wheat of God's saints reaped and gathered into heaven then the grapes of the peoples who reject God's rule gathered into the winepress of God's wrath. A 1,600 furlong river of blood to the depth of the horse bridles spoke of the just judgment of God falling upon every citizen of the kingdom of Antichrist without exception. You would be wise to ask of whose kingdom you are a citizen. The kingdom of Christ or that of Antichrist? God's kingdom or Satan's? The message is simple and stark; if you are not sealed with the conversion mark of the gospel of Christ you can only be a citizen of the kingdom of Antichrist. But today is still the day of salvation. Christ bids any and all who hear his voice through gospel preaching, or perhaps through the words written here, to come to him for rest.

Now in the fifth vision, we see the end in even greater detail described by seven vials of divine wrath in retribution for sin. Later, in chapters 17 to 19, there is more detail given of the end before leading up to the glory and bliss of the new heaven and earth, and the new Jerusalem. But for now, let us seek to understand the message of this fifth vision.

In Revelation 15:1 we read of John seeing 'another sign in heaven, great and marvellous'. Thus the detail of the fifth vision (sign) is introduced. All the works of God are described as 'great and marvellous'. His gospel of redemption by the blood of Christ is 'marvellous in the eyes' of those who are the objects of salvation, and supplies the theme of their song in glory (v. 3). But, as salvation from wrath is marvellous, so too is the punishment of sin, for it too is entirely in accord with the holy character of God. The great and marvellous sign consists of seven angels having the seven last plagues which fulfil, or complete, the wrath of God. These glorious beings hold vials, symbolical vessels, containing the balancing judgments of God to destroy all sin and rebellion from this created order.

Skip over verses 2 to 4 for now and go to verse 5. The angels come out of the heavenly abode of God and in verse 7 they are given the seven golden vials full of God's wrath by one of the four beasts. We know that the four beasts speak of creation. Perhaps this echoes Romans 8:22 where Paul tells us 'For we know that the whole creation groaneth and travaileth in pain together until now.' Creation 'wants' the curse of sin and rebellion against its creator to be ended and removed.

In chapter 16 verse 1 God commands the angels to go and pour out their vials of wrath upon the earth. The seven are poured out on the earth itself, the sea, fresh water, the sun, the 'seat of the beast', on the River Euphrates and at Armageddon, the scene of the final battle. In a sense there is nothing new here that the seals and trumpets have not already revealed. Do not forget that the seals, trumpets and vials must not be interpreted as sequential. In some ways all of them have already started, but the distinctive thing about the vials is they clearly speak of finality. This is the end of God's judgments, the culmination of his retribution for sin in this space-time creation.

The loosing of the seals brought harm to a quarter of humanity, the trumpets brought harm to a third, a greater proportion, the vials speak of complete harm. In verses 1 to 9 the first four vials are poured out on the earth, the sea, fresh water and the sun, rather like the first four trumpets. They stop this world from being a place able to support natural life. But whereas the destruction was partial with the trumpets, now with the vials the destruction of life is complete.

The kingdom of Antichrist, described in detail in Revelation 13, has the full support of all who are not sealed with the conversion seal of God's Holy Spirit. The conversion of Christ's people is evidenced by their sanctification by the Spirit and belief of the truth (2 Thessalonians 2:13). All but Christ's believing people relish the material comforts of the kingdom of Antichrist, they support its godless political cooperation, they work for its economic prosperity and cherish the wonders of science, technology and medicine the False Prophet uses to seduce them[18]. But

---

[18] It is not that I am saying that we, as believers, do not make use of some of these things to our benefit but we view them as what they really are. We know they

the first four vials completely destroy these things and, with them, they destroy the world's capacity to support life.

In verses 10 and 11, the fifth vial darkens the rule of Antichrist so the peoples of the world no longer worship him because of the pain experienced by the darkening of his rule (the seat of the beast). Yet they still do not bow to the rule of God; they refuse to repent of their deeds of rebellion.

Then in verses 12 to 14 the sixth vial removes all borders between Antichrist's kingdom of false religion, Christendom, and the rest of the world outside of the influence of the first seal; the White Horse of the gospel that disrupted Satan's intentions. We saw these borders being removed in the sixth trumpet in Revelation 9:13-21. In a way, the worldwide unity without Christ for which Satan has striven in his kingdom of Antichrist is achieved by the pouring out of the sixth vial. It removes national borders as we see to some extent today and yet, rather than uniting all nations together against God, it only foments global conflict. This is reinforced by verse 13 where we see three unclean spirits like frogs coming out of the mouths of the dragon, the beast and the false prophet, doubtless Satan's infernal trinity, seeking to mimic the Trinity of God. They work miracles whilst doing their Antichrist missionary work in an effort to unite the world for the impending final battle, but as much as they evidently try, they seem constantly to be frustrated in their purpose.

Let us skip verse 15 for now and look at verses 16 to 21. Here the seventh vial is poured out in the form of the battle of Armageddon. This is the final battle which completes the judgment of God on the kingdom of Satan and his Antichrist. The significance of the name is in its reference to Mount Megiddo near the valley of Jezreel which was a great battlefield where Israel confronted and defeated the enemies of God. In Judges 5:19 we see Deborah and Barak victorious there. In Ezekiel 38 we see mention of Gog and Magog, the heathen nations to the east of the River Euphrates. Towards the end of that chapter a great conflict is pictured between Israel as the people of God and the kingdoms of Gog and Magog as his enemies. Ezekiel 38:22 rings very close to the wording of the end of Revelation 16 as it speaks of the same battle. This is the final destruction of this space-time creation as the stronghold of Satan and Antichrist. Therefore, verse 17 says, a great voice from out of the temple of heaven from the throne of God announces, 'It is done!'.

---

promise good without the necessary satisfaction of God's justice in Christ's atonement and, therefore, we do not worship them or what they represent.

To be caught up in that final, complete, retribution of God against all sin will be terrible. The soul with any sense of its guilt and the judgment to come surely must be filled with dreadful foreboding and cry, "What must I do to be saved from that certain fate?" Praise God there is a clear answer. On the cross of Calvary the Son of God, the Lord Jesus Christ, cried out, "It is finished!" (John 19:30). These words are basically the same as 'it is done'. At Calvary he bore the sin of his people, whom the Father gave him in sovereign, electing grace before time began. Divine retribution for their sin fell on Christ as their substitute to the full extent of the justice of God. Now his people have no appointment (Hebrews 9:27) at the final pouring out of the complete retribution pictured in Revelation 16. His people stand safe upon the ground where the wrath of God already has fallen, in the person of his Son. No wonder those who believe the Son say so willingly, "Praise the Lord, O my soul!"

But for all the rest who are outside of Christ on that day, the full extent of the justice of God will be satisfied as his wrath falls on them, and then as at Calvary, it will be declared, "It is done!"

Revelation 16:18-21 describes in symbol and picture a dreadful destruction of this world at the end. The cities, centres of civilisation, sundry geographical features, all of it is completely destroyed. It speaks of 'great hail', in fact 50kg hailstones! Could the warning be any clearer? There is no need to speculate and quibble about the interpretation of the details, just acknowledge that a violent end is coming to this world and all upon it who reject the rule of God. Do not wait for more proof of this. The vials stir up blasphemy among men, not repentance and faith.

Christ And His People
We have seen clear indications in previous visions of how God's saints increasingly will find life difficult because of opposition from the kingdom of Antichrist as the end approaches. This they must endure without precise knowledge of how long it will go on. Therefore, in the midst of the gruesome details of the sixth and seventh vials, Christ, it seems, puts in a word of comfort and assurance to his saints (v. 15). He is making clear what is going to happen as this world is brought to an end, but he reminds his people he is coming for them. Before the end Christ will come as unexpectedly as a thief and take his people to heaven just as he told his disciples he would. 'Be ye therefore ready also: for the Son of man cometh at an hour when ye think not' (Luke 12:40). We have already seen the wheat harvested before the grapes are cast into the winepress of God's wrath and the witnesses in chapter 11 were taken up to heaven before the seventh trumpet blew. Christ will remove his elect

from this world before the seven vials reach their full and final intensity. Immediately before Armageddon when the unbelieving world is finally destroyed, Christ will take his people home to glory.

Our Saviour counsels his people to watch in patient anticipation whilst keeping their garments. What garments are these? Surely the garments of salvation of which Isaiah 61:10 speaks. Strive to stay close to Christ, to walk in his way, and be assured your destiny is heavenly glory, away from all the dreadful judgments about to fall upon this world.

Now, look back at Revelation 15:2-4 that we skipped over earlier. What is it that awaits the people of God? It is what is pictured in these verses, God's people in glory. There is a sea of glass mingled with fire. Remember Israel beside the Red Sea (Exodus 15)? They were saved from the clutches of the Egyptians whom they saw destroyed before their eyes. The Red Sea that saved them also destroyed their enemies. It is the same with Christ. He is the savour of life unto life for his people but the savour of death unto death for his enemies (2 Corinthians 2:16). Simeon said of the infant Jesus, "this child is set for the fall and rising of many in Israel" (Luke 2:34). At the Red Sea everything that oppressed and persecuted Israel of old was destroyed in their sight and so it shall be for God's people in glory. They will see their triumph over the beast, his image, his mark and his number, indeed over everything that signified the kingdom of Satan and his Antichrist.

Continuing the analogy with Israel and Egypt; just as Moses leading Israel out of bondage was typical of Christ saving his church from the bondage of sin, so too, the Israelites' singing the song of Moses (Exodus 15:1) is typical of the Israel of God (Galatians 6:16) singing the song of Moses and the Lamb in glory. It is a song of triumph and praise for God in his total and final victory over Satan.

Are you ready for his return? Are you watching and waiting, patiently anticipating his imminent return? Looking for Christ and to Christ? Or do you dismiss the things we have been considering as implausible scaremongering? If it is the latter, tell me, if you can, what in the past has led you to distrust his word? What has he ever said that has failed the test of prophetic scrutiny? You will not find anything. Why then should his word lie to you now?

Chapter 20

The Woman Named Babylon

Revelation 17

The fifth vision in chapters 15 and 16 showed us the end of history, the end of this space-time creation. It culminated in the pouring out of the seventh vial of God's wrath against sin resulting in the battle of Armageddon. This is some sort of world-wide conflict between the forces of false Christianity, what we have called Christendom, and the peoples of Gog and Magog. In a way, it is the end of the unfolding of God's plan, his seven-sealed book. God has destroyed everything of Satan's kingdom of Antichrist and established his own unrivalled kingdom of peace and true righteousness.

But though it was the end of the loosing of the seals, the sounding of the trumpets and the pouring out of the vials of wrath, it is not the end of the book of Revelation. We have noted how the visions provide different perspectives, often of the same situation. Well, in a similar manner, they can be viewed as different reports of the same news event. When you watch a television news bulletin of some major event or disaster, the main headline report is often followed by additional reports by other reporters giving their own individual perspective on the event. Recall, if you can, the occasion when terrorists flew planes into the twin towers of the World Trade Center in New York and into the Pentagon. For days and weeks afterwards, new reports providing different perspectives on aspects of the calamity continued to emerge. In the same way, I believe the sixth vision of the book of Revelation, comprising chapters 17 to 19, provides a different perspective of the report of the final battle given at the end of chapter 16. We are taken back to see aspects of the things leading to and culminating in the final battle.

All scripture speaks of God saving his elect people out of the kingdom of Satan and the coming of his own glorious kingdom. It all reports the same theme of Jesus Christ and him crucified. The message is the same but it is described by different reports. Sometimes it is scenes from history, sometimes poetry, prophecy, narrative and epistle is used. Revelation 17 is another view of the same great message.

137

The Woman Named Babylon

Following the account of the final end of all things in this created order, we are told more detail of the circumstances that contributed to the final destruction. Our reporter filing his news report is one of the seven angels who had the seven vials of wrath to pour out. What we have here in verses 1 to 6 is his report which concerns a great whore that sits upon many waters.

A whore is an immoral woman, a prostitute. She is unfaithful to any one man. She is adulterous and makes a career of attracting and acquiring multiple sexual partners. Here she is pictured as being buoyed up by waters which we see from verse 15 are the peoples of the world. Verse 2 describes her as being in league with world powers and of her influence causing a drunkenness, a distortion of vision and loss of rational wisdom. Obviously, she is opposed to the holiness of God and is deserving of judgment (v. 1).

In verses 3 and 4 we see a vision of this woman in her natural environment. She is in a 'wilderness' but this time it is not a wilderness of separation from the world, like the place where God put his church in chapter 12. This is a wilderness of godless sinfulness, the abode of those without God and without hope in the world (Ephesians 2:12). John sees her sitting on a scarlet coloured beast, gorgeously clothed, expensively adorned with jewels, but the golden cup she held contained vile things.

Her name is 'Mystery' (v. 5), something hidden and not obvious. A name in scripture is associated closely with character and although she has the appearance of a glamorous woman, she has the character of a city, the abominable city of Babylon. In verse 6 we see her drunk with an excess of the blood of the saints. The translation gives the impression John is almost seduced by the appearance of this woman but a better translation would be he is astonished, he is shocked at what he is looking at. But why is he so shocked?

He has seen a woman in a previous vision (Revelation 12:1). That woman was clearly the true church of Christ, the people of God of the Old and New Testaments, from whom Christ came according to the flesh. She was also the bride of Christ whom he came to earth to sanctify and cleanse so he might present her to himself a glorious church, not having spot, or wrinkle, or any such thing; but that it should be holy and without blemish (Ephesians 5:27). Now, when John sees another vision of a woman, he expects it to be Christ's bride again; but this woman is drunk with the blood of the saints and her name and her true character, is Babylon.

138

We have noted previously how in Genesis 11, Nimrod, the rebellious panther, initiated the kingdom of Antichrist at Babel, with its tower of aspiration to reach heaven but without the satisfaction of divine justice. God inflicted a mortal wound to the head of that objective when he confounded languages and prevented worldwide unification of mankind in opposition to the rule of God. We saw the wound again in the vision of Revelation 13:3 but there we saw the deadly wound had been healed. The historical outworking of the healing is seen in the great empires of the ancient world, those of Babylon, Medo-Persia, Greece and Rome. Today we see the same thing in organisations like the United Nations, the European Union and similar world bodies formed ostensibly for unity and freedom of international movement. We see it also, I suggested, in modern computer applications like instant translation tools. The point to remember is that the healing of the wound always stands for oppression and persecution of the true people of God (see v. 14). Nevertheless, Babylon will be ultimately defeated. Its fall is repeated in scripture. Isaiah wrote, 'Babylon is fallen, is fallen'(Isaiah 21:9). It is repeated in Revelation 14:8 and 16:19 and we shall see it again in Revelation 18:2. The downfall of all false religion is writ large.

So then, what at first sight looks like God's pure church is, in fact, a whore named Babylon. In Revelation 11 we saw John being told to measure the temple, to mark out the true people of God. He was only to measure the central part of the temple but not bother with the temple court or the rest of the city of Jerusalem. It all, the whole of the temple precincts looked superficially like the place where the people of God resided, but in truth God's true people were only those in the core of the temple. The temple court, the rest of Jerusalem and wider Israel/Judea are in reality Babylon; they are Sodom and Egypt (Revelation 11:8) where the prophets were killed and Christ was crucified. This rings true with the Old Testament picture of Israel seeming to be God's people in the world but repeatedly playing the harlot with idols and every form of false religion. This picture is presented vividly in the prophecy of Hosea.

Recognising The Woman Named Babylon

This woman that the angel showed to John in Revelation 17 is the 'church' as she appears on earth to most people of the world. It is Christendom with all its outward signs. The media recognises it as Christ's church. They are seduced by its buildings, its ministers in their ornate robes, its structure and organisation, its use of the 'bible', its sacraments and its works, but they completely fail to look for effectual salvation. My wife and I visited Rome recently as noted in an earlier chapter. All around us, among the impressive historical architecture, were thousands of people who were convinced they were in the 'Eternal City', the headquarters of 'Christianity'. The Vatican, the pope, the cardinals, priests and nuns are there, some in great numbers, but they all utterly deny 'Jesus Christ is come in the flesh' (1 John 4:1-3). That probably surprises you. You are certain they believe Jesus was born at Bethlehem, after all look at the fuss they make at Christmas and Easter. But that is a million miles from believing and testifying that everything the Old Testament prophesied concerning the promised Messiah and his redemption of the elect of God, is fulfilled in Jesus the man born at Bethlehem. That is what it is to confess Jesus Christ is come in the flesh.

Christendom, represented in Revelation 17 by the whore named Babylon, despises the sovereign grace of God, it hates particular redemption and it sees no need for blood redemption because it has no God-given sense of sin. It is idolatry pure and simple. It is unbiblical, an invented religion as can be seen by even a superficial comparison of its creeds and practices with the clear teaching of the Bible. It wants to be known as the bride of Christ but it blatantly commits spiritual fornication with the kingdom of Antichrist.

Let us not limit it to Roman Catholicism. Many churches are in the same boat of denying the key essentials of the true gospel. Today, so-called evangelicals are just as compromised and spiritually adulterous, despite many of them until quite recently appearing to stand for truth. In the last few decades there is clear evidence of a drift into the practices and doctrines of heresy. Even those who talk of 'redeeming blood' flatter to deceive. The blood of which they speak is universal in its redeeming extent and therefore ineffectual to save a single sinner[19]. They offer a gospel aimed at man's free-will using every worldly enticement they can to influence their hearers to join and support them. Some who claim to be faithful in holding to the grace of the gospel deny it completely by enforcing legal obedience in every quarter of their practice. They dance to the music of heresy and their flirtation entices to spiritual adultery. Fearing isolation in a 'day of small things' they embrace ecumenical associations as 'fellowship'. But Christ is not the centre of their creed, their preaching, their message or their devotion (Philippians 3:3).

---

[19] If Christ's blood paid the sin-debt of everyone without exception then no one has anything to answer for at the bar of God's justice, yet that is patently not so. Many are already in hell and daily thousands go the same way. To suggest Christ paid their sin-debt yet they end up in hell is blasphemous to the glorious name and finished work of Christ.

I ask each reader, do you attend a church? Does it look like a true church, like a local manifestation of the true body of Christ? Or is its name really Babylon? Does it 'keep the commandments of God and the faith of Jesus'? Or is it flirting with idols? Is it compromised with Balaam's doctrine which taught Israel to commit fornication even though some of its statements appear as the truth? If yes, then heed the call of Revelation 18:4 and 'come out of her my people'!

The Mystery Unfolded
Do you find the meaning of this sixth vision shocking? Were you expecting a great revival in the church before the end? Perhaps what you thought was the true church in its 21st Century manifestation is now revealed to be a whore committing spiritual fornication with the kingdom of Antichrist? Well, in verse 7, the angel says he is going to tell John the mystery of the woman and the beast that carried her.

Verses 8 to 13 read like a convoluted riddle, none more so than verse 11. Why does it have to be so complex? I guess it is because we are at the interface between the eternal, unknowable things of God, and the physical manifestation of God's decrees in this space-time creation. We need to treat these words with reverence and respect. In a very real sense, the history of the world is bound up in these words. I will attempt to put down some clear markers to help us understand, but in the final analysis, do not be concerned if you do not understand everything or even most of it. Remember Revelation 1:3; the blessing comes from hearing and keeping, not from understanding every detail.

Beginning in verse 8, John is reminded of the beast he saw. It was real then 1,900 years ago when John was writing, but it was not as it had once been. This is the same beast pictured in the vision of chapter 9, the beast from the bottomless pit, and also in Revelation 13:1 arising from the sea. Its historical manifestation was seen at Babel as a unified world-wide political power reaching for heaven without the satisfaction of divine justice. There it was given a deadly wound when the languages were confused and so the text says that it is not, i.e. not now, when John was writing in his day, as it once had been. As the beast of Revelation 13:1 it represents unified political power and it is supported by the second beast from the earth with his signs and wonders. The peoples of the world, as verse 8 confirms, are filled with wonder; they worship the beast, all except the people of God, his elect, whose names are written in the book of life from the foundation of the world.

In verse 9, the seven heads of the beast are seven mountains. Mountains in scripture are often representative of kingdoms and earthly

141

powers. The woman who is a whore sits on these earthly powers; that is, she gets her support from the peoples and nations of the world. Have you ever heard the powers or spokesmen of political Christendom say anything to undermine the false church? No, they support her!

In verse 10 the seven kings are world empires. Remember when John was writing the book of Revelation it was the time of the Roman empire, so we read 'and one is'. Think of the five empires that came before the Roman empire. Three of them correlate closely with Nebuchadnezzar's dream of Daniel 2. He, representing the Babylonian Empire, is the golden head, then Medo-Persia is the silver breast and arms, Greece is the brass belly and thighs, and Rome is the iron legs with feet mixed with clay. The great empires before Babylon were Assyria and before that Egypt. This is not fiction. Anyone visiting London can visit the British Museum and see numerous artefacts from the Assyrian Empire. You wander those galleries and look at things 3,000 years old and more. The common characteristic of all of these empires is they sought, albeit by force of arms, to achieve political unity stretching as widely across the world as they could, like Nimrod's Babel, but they all fell short of their aims. They fell short because their objective was actually Satan's, and God loosed his seals and trumpets to frustrate him. That seemed to make sense did it not? But it is not over yet. We still need to decipher verse 11.

Quickly skip forward and look at verses 12 and 13. At the time John was writing there were ten kingdoms yet to come. Their power will be relatively fleeting, one hour, but they will be of one mind. Could this be the old kingdom of Nimrod's Babel forming again as an eighth world empire (v. 11) but actually a confederation of the ten kingdoms which constitute the seventh world empire? Stop, think, go back and read that again. Then think a bit more. Are there any clear signs of it today? I am not sure, but it could be that it is forming. Certainly, all the ten kingdoms support the beast, the kingdom of Antichrist. He promises peace without divine justice and without the blood to accomplish it. This humanist attainment of worldly peace and harmony is what we see today as the general philosophy of the world around us. Let me give you an example. I listen to the radio and I hear accolades to the memory of recently deceased broadcaster Sir Terry Wogan, someone regarded universally as a 'lovely man'. Personally, I could not help but be charmed by his conviviality, but he stood for human goodness with no need for the blood of Christ. Likewise, I hear Joan Bakewell revered as a wonderful example of intelligent, rational, feeling humanity, but again she would let you know clearly her contempt for the concept of the gospel of grace. This is the modern empire in which we are living and I feel there is scope for it to become much worse before the end. Satan's intention is for the woman, adulterous Christendom, to seduce world powers so that there is one, final, united kingdom of Antichrist promising eternal peace without satisfaction of divine justice.

In verse 14 we hear of war between these kingdoms, the eighth empire and the Lamb of God. The Lamb overcomes them. How does he achieve the victory? In verse 16 we read the kings who once supported the whore now hate her. In verse 17 we learn they hate her because God has put it in their hearts to fulfil his will. Perhaps we can see a parallel here, too. Just at the moment when Christendom imagined it was supreme in the world, there is a massive turning away from even nominal 'Christian religion'. The Lamb is in the process of overcoming the kingdom of Antichrist using the very means Satan contrived to achieve what he thought would be his victory. His own weapons are used against him. Is that not remarkably like what occurred at Calvary when Satan was defeated in the very moment he was sure he had triumphed.

Application
No doubt there is much more to see in this, but the key in verse 14 is that Christ and his called, chosen, faithful people are victorious. The whore ends up desolate, naked, burned and eaten (v. 16). Examine your situation and ask whether your 'church' is in fact a manifestation of the whore named Babylon, and if so, come out of her my people before it is too late (Revelation 18:4).

Chapter 21

The Fall Of Babylon

Revelation 18

The book of Revelation was given to the last living apostle, John, around the year AD 95. The New Testament church was suffering great persecution. It had spread widely through the Mediterranean world but it was far from converting the whole world. Some might have wondered if it would survive or whether the whole Christian movement would slowly peter out. Christ had promised that the gates of hell would not prevail against his church but the Roman Empire must have seemed to many to be prevailing fairly well against it, with Nero's savage oppression. To comfort them, God gave the Revelation to his persecuted people so they might see a heavenly perspective on world history from the Fall in Eden to its ultimate destiny.

What has been revealed so far is how Satan has constantly tried to establish his worldwide kingdom of Antichrist, a combination of hatred for the principle of God's righteousness and of divine justice. Throughout history he has sought to mimic God's way. His infernal trinity of Satan, the Beast and the False Prophet have set up his false church depicted as a harlot woman named Babylon (Revelation 17:5). She aspires to heaven without the satisfaction of divine justice for sin. Satan began with Babel and its tower in Genesis 11, and followed that with the great world empires of ancient history, but God constantly frustrated his purposes with the seals, trumpets and vials of wrath we have seen in earlier chapters. None of Satan's attempts at worldwide unity with godless purpose were allowed to reach full maturity. Believers in AD 95 and in the years following, were encouraged to continue in the faith by the perspectives Revelation supplied of the coming defeat of anti-Christian political power and godless worldly society. Satan himself, whose schemes these were has but a little time left. But the picture of Revelation is not yet complete for there are still five more chapters to come.

Revelation 18 opens with 'after these things', meaning the things described in chapter 17. We need to be reminded of them to set chapter 18 in its proper context.

War And Peace

In Tolstoy's epic novel of that name, the wonderful experience of peace at the end is preceded by intense, bitter warfare and suffering. In a similar way, God's believing people have to go through a time of war before they reach the eternal peace of heaven. We were told in Revelation 17:14 that 'these shall make war with the Lamb'. Who are the 'these' that shall make war? They are earthly political, economic, philosophical, academic powers and peoples, and the false religion borne along by them. How do they make war with the Lamb? They do it by attacking and persecuting the Lamb's church for Jesus said 'Inasmuch as ye have done it unto one of the least of these my brethren, ye have done it unto me' (Matthew 25:40). At times the attacks have been very physical and saints have been martyred for the cause of Christ, but mostly the attacks are in the form of ideas, philosophies, and society's values turning right and wrong upside down. We see it all around us today in materialistic, evolutionary thinking and in modern corrupt morality that has normalised sodomy and trans-gender perversions. It has permeated every aspect of civilised life and brought radical and rapid changes to family life, education and business making it increasingly difficult for believers to abide by the precepts of the gospel whilst, of necessity, interacting with the world around.

Be under no delusion; if you follow Christ you will constantly be in a fight with the world and its false religion. Do not ever try to make peace with it by compromising the gospel. As the body of Christ in this world, the church must fill up the sufferings of Christ (Colossians 1:24). But do not despair at the situation for it is a very uneven contest. As soon as we read of this war we read 'the Lamb shall overcome them'. Christ is supreme; he is King of kings and Lord of lords. Of course they cannot win. He overcomes them as the Lamb. The Lamb is the sin-atoning sacrifice who has disarmed Satan in his accusations of the brethren. Christ, the Lamb, overcomes all. Some are overcome as children of wrath by his saving grace in time, and the rest shall be overcome by his strict justice in the Day of Judgment at the end of time.

Called, Chosen, Faithful

In Revelation 17:14 we read of the people with the Lamb who overcomes his enemies. They are described as called, chosen and faithful. Christ's

146

people are with him at all times. How comforting that must have been in AD 95! But it also speaks powerfully to us today as the end approaches. Throughout the trials of this war with the world and false religion, Christ is with his people and they with him. His people are with him by reason of their election before the beginning of time. They are with him by betrothal as when he stood as the Surety of his bride in the covenant of grace. They are with him by virtue of the salvation he has accomplished for them at Calvary. They are with him experimentally by the Holy Spirit's indwelling of them.

Those who are with the Lamb in his war with Satan's kingdom of Antichrist are with him because God in sovereign grace chose them in Christ. He called them with his name in eternal union and called them in time with the Holy Spirit's irresistible call, making them faithful by giving them new life in the new birth. Thus eternally united with the Lamb of God, his people shall overcome the kingdom of Antichrist irrespective of the trials through which they must pass before the end.

How Do They Overcome?
In Revelation 17:16, 17 we read of the ten horns on the beast coming to hate the whore and effectively destroy her. This whore who previously was borne along by worldly political powers shall come to be hated by those same powers. I believe this is telling us how God will use even the powers of Antichrist's kingdom to disrupt that kingdom. Just as he did at Babel when the confused languages caused instant disunity. God will disrupt Satan's plans for worldwide unity of Christ-less aspiration for heaven. I believe we are seeing clear signs of this today as the political world of the last 20 or 30 years casts off most of the constraints of the morality of Christendom.

The woman who reigned over the kings of the earth (v. 18) is the very one those kings will hate. Babylon, which is her name (Revelation 17:5), is coming to an end. Chapter 18:1-3 provides the announcement of its downfall. This tells us this world and everything it involves is coming to a definite end. Its philosophies, culture, skills, trade, its society, its civilisation along with its comforts, charms, beauty and delights, is all coming to an abrupt end. How can we be so sure? A powerful angel announced it from heaven. I am strongly inclined to believe this is Christ, the Messenger of the Covenant making the announcement. He is God, and particularly he is the manifestation of the unknowable God to fallen man, and he is the one by whom God makes this announcement. There is no higher authority, there is no more certain pronouncement to be fulfilled.

Even as I am writing this, my unbelieving flesh is telling me to doubt it as, no doubt, yours is too. But thank God, at the new birth his Spirit gave me a new man, one with ears to hear what this old man of flesh is unable to hear. The new man is utterly convinced this announcement is true. Babylon, the embodiment of worldly, false religion, is indeed fallen, it is just a matter of time until we see it actually happen.

The Fall Of Babylon
Everything that has rebelled against the justice of God (v. 3) will be brought to a sudden end, in one hour, as it says in verse 10. We are not told here exactly how the end will be implemented but the end is no less certain because of that. Be in no doubt, this world and all that opposes Christ and his people, its society, culture and false religion, will end.
In verse 5 we read the sin of the world will end. God will say 'enough!' Just as he did with the world of Noah's day and with Sodom and the cities of the plain, the longsuffering of God will reach its limit. In verse 6, God's response to the sin of the world and the kingdom of Antichrist is strict justice, exactly the payment required by sin's debt to the law. It is what is meant by the word 'double'. It does not mean twice as much but rather a mirror image, an exact equivalence.

In verse 7 we are told Babylon's presumption of continuing opulent living will be suddenly cut short. Is it not graphically illustrated in history and archaeology by the real city of Babylon? God pronounced it would remain a ruin after its historical destruction, and so it has. Despite conflict you can visit the bustling city of Damascus today, but Babylon is just an archaeological site in the desert of Iraq. Similarly, God said animal sacrifices in the temple would end once Christ had fulfilled all the Old Testament pictures, so they did in AD 70 never to be reinstated. Note this well, and do not doubt it. The same and only God who pronounced the fall of ancient Babylon and the end of the temple sacrifices is the one who here in Revelation 18 announces the end of spiritual Babylon.

Suddenly in verses 8 and 9 we see the joy of this Christ-rejecting world being turned to great sorrow because they see the end of everything that sustained them in their rejection of God's rule. Read on down to verse 19 and see how all the world's trade in coveted things comes to an abrupt end with devastating impact on those who thrived by it. What a contrast is drawn between the lamentation of the kingdom of Antichrist for the fall of Babylon, and, in verse 20, the call for God's people to rejoice at it. The martyrs' cry of, "how long?" in Revelation 6:10 is answered here in verse 20. We are told God has avenged his persecuted people on those who oppressed and martyred them. This is not vindictive spite, on the contrary, it is simply strict justice applied. As verse 24 says, the evidence is easily found of Babylon's offences against the kingdom of Christ and she is rewarded, 'double unto her double according to her works' (v. 6).

The end will be violent (v. 21). It is pictured metaphorically as a great millstone being cast into the sea but no details are given. Nevertheless, it reinforces the picture given at the end of Revelation 16 of the Battle of Armageddon and essentially it is speaking of exactly the same end. Verses 22 and 23 portray a scene of devastation following a great disaster. This is the end of all worldly culture; its craft, industry, society, and marriage for the procreation of children, even the end of candle-light is pictured. Everything by which Satan and his kingdom of Antichrist deceived all the nations is coming to a sudden end.

The Call To God's People

While the world is cast into deep lamentation over the downfall of Babylon, God's people are called upon to rejoice (v. 20) because God's justice is done and is clearly seen to be done. Nevertheless, it is all still future, it is still to happen at the end of this world and we who are living here and now are yet to see these things come to pass at the end of time. So, in preparation, what ought we to do now?

In verse 4, God's people, who believe Christ, who trust him alone for salvation from the just consequences of their sins, are told to come out of Babylon. In other words, believers are told to be separated from the world of Satan and his Antichrist. But how are we to do that? This world has things we need to sustain life; we have no option but to do business in it, to trade and interact with its peoples. Some might think we should set up monasteries to provide controlled isolation, or emigrate to a remote island where we can govern ourselves according to God's word like the Pilgrim Fathers did in emigrating to America in 1620. Unfortunately, the record of these and all similar 'worldly separation' enterprises is that sinners quickly pollute any clean environment with the fruits of their sinfulness. At the flood God swept away every sinner except Noah and the seven people with him in the ark, but in a few generations their descendants had set up Babylon. So how ought we to respond to the call of Revelation 18:4?

In the time of literal Babylon, when the Jews for their idolatry were taken into 70 years of captivity in Babylon, God's prophets, Isaiah and Jeremiah, repeatedly called for separation. At the end of the captivity, Zechariah wrote 'deliver thyself, O Zion, that dwellest with the daughter of Babylon' (Zechariah 2:7). How are we to heed this call? Believers are to be in the world but not of the world. We are to live in Sodom for the necessities of life as Lot did until the angel took him out, but unlike his wife, be sure that our heart is not in Sodom. We are to partake of what the world provides as vital sustenance for the body in the form of food, drink and air; on the strength of God's word we can even enjoy what does not defile. But do not rest your hopes on it, do not invest your treasures in it, rather strive to lay up treasure in heaven. Hear what John writes in his first epistle, 'Love not the world, neither the things that are in the world. If any man love the world, the love of the Father is not in him. For all that is in the world, the lust of the flesh, and the lust of the eyes, and the pride of life, is not of the Father, but is of the world. And the world passeth away, and the lust thereof: but he that doeth the will of God abideth for ever' (1 John 2:15-17).

There are many who profess to be Christians in our day who think they have a responsibility to influence the world and its false religion for good. Some in erstwhile evangelical churches acknowledge their modern gospel is flawed and unscriptural, but they imagine by staying and supporting the institution, they will be able to have an influence for good that might heal it and steer it back to the truth. Many years ago I used to think like that myself, but it is a fallacy. You are not able to heal what God has said he will destroy. It is coming to an end along with the rest of Babylon and the kingdom of Antichrist. The call of God's word is for his true believing people to separate from it before it is too late. The same applies to society in general. Do not waste time in futile political campaigning to get society to conform more to God's word. Rather, bear witness to what God has done for you in forgiving your sins and giving you a solid hope of eternity based on divine justice satisfied by God's Son.

Think of it like this; you are a passenger on the Titanic and your 'cabin' is the ship's only working lifeboat. Go out and about round the ship. Look at its opulence, its high society, the ingenuity and skill that built it. Admire its sea-going performance, enjoy its food and drink and admire the views. But know for sure, it is destined to hit an iceberg and sink with the loss of all but those in your lifeboat. Your lifeboat is Christ and his justice-satisfying blood. As you live in this world and interact with it as you must always keep this in the front of your mind. By God's Spirit within, by Christ's constraining love, by God's gift of faith (Revelation 12:14), inhabit that wilderness place of God (Revelation 12:6). There he promises to sustain his people, separate from Babylon and its sins 'that ye receive not of her plagues' (Revelation 18:4).

Chapter 22

The Marriage Of The Lamb

Revelation 19:1-10

As we have moved through the book of Revelation, we have seen the visions progressively reveal more detail concerning the end of this creation. In a sense they have all shown differing perspectives of the same things but the later visions provide more detail about the end of Satan's kingdom and the glories of God's. As we near the end of the book we see brighter and clearer views of heaven itself.

The sixth vision of Revelation began at the start of chapter 17 and we now see its completion in chapter 19. It began when one of the seven angels who poured out the vials of the wrath of God showed John the judgment of the great whore, the gorgeously arrayed woman whose name is Babylon. The angel showed us the end of Babylon, the end of the beast and the image worshipped by the peoples of the world. He showed us the downfall of Satan's kingdom of Antichrist with its worldly philosophy, morals, politics, pseudo-science and religion. We saw the end of all who thrived in Babylon. Since the Fall in Eden, this world has been the battleground between Satan and God for supreme lordship. Satan strives for lordship by promising men eternal security based on the lie that divine justice can be ignored. God declares he will be Lord of all things but only on the basis of righteousness and divine justice satisfied. This is only accomplished by the blood of God's Son for the people of his choice.

If you believe the gospel and your trust is in Christ alone you know God will triumph. His justice will be honoured and Satan will be forever defeated. God's people, including you, will be with him forever in eternal happiness. But we need patience to wait while we are still here in this life. Patience is a mark of true faith, Paul says, 'Remembering without ceasing your work of faith, and labour of love, and patience of hope in our Lord Jesus Christ' (1 Thessalonians 1:3). We are like the peoples of the free world in early 1945 waiting for the end of WW2, knowing soon there will be celebration and the end of all conflict. Or perhaps it is more like waiting for the day of a wedding; all the planning is done and everything is booked and ordered. However, in this case as we wait we are provided with a video of the wedding before we experience it! That is what we have here in Revelation 19. Let us run the video now by following the vision as it is given to John.

What is the situation now when Babylon has been finally destroyed, as we saw it reported in chapters 17 and 18? There has been dreadful pain and loss, anguish and sorrow for all who thrived and rejoiced in Babylon. However, for all who suffered as Christ's true sheep in Babylon, the scene is now transferred to heaven.

Much People In Heaven
John hears a great voice of much people in heaven. These are the same as the multitude no man can number in Revelation 7:9. They have arrived finally on the distant shore. What Christ willed the night before he was crucified has been fulfilled. 'Father, I will that they also, whom thou hast given me, be with me where I am that they may behold my glory' (John 17:24). Having hoped for it, and waited patiently for it, there they are in heaven, in God's holy presence, in the inner temple sanctuary. Though they lived here in bodies of flesh, now they must be without sin in heaven for 'there shall in no wise enter into it any thing that defileth, neither whatsoever worketh abomination, or maketh a lie: but they which are written in the Lamb's book of life' (Revelation 21:27). This 'much people' are those chosen in Christ before the foundation of the world (Ephesians 1:4; 2 Timothy 1:9). They were sinners but have been justified by Christ, made the righteousness of God in him (2 Corinthians 5:21). They were law-breakers who were redeemed from the law's curse by Christ being made a curse for them (Galatians 3:13). Now they are fully qualified to partake of heaven (Colossians 1:12). Do you have a good hope you are numbered among them? Have you believed the Son of God? Has the Holy Spirit given you faith to trust Christ? Are you counted worthy to partake of communion by virtue of your discernment of the Lord's broken body and shed blood purchasing your redemption from sin's just penalty? Are you numbered with God's true circumcision who worship God in the Spirit, rejoice in Christ Jesus, and have no confidence in the flesh? (Philippians 3:3). Then be assured you are among this much people in heaven. Look at the 'video' of his record in these verses of Revelation 19 and see yourself there.

What are they all doing? They are praising God with a loud voice. They are extolling God's glory seen most clearly in his grace to sinners (Exodus 33:18), and in the salvation he has accomplished. They praise God for his unrivalled omnipotence and his satisfaction of justice in the death Christ died. But they praise him also for the eternal retribution (v. 3) inflicted on all who rebelled against him. The whole of the redeemed church of God, pictured by twenty-four elders, and the whole of the restored creation, the four beasts, give willing praise to God.

So we come to verse 7 and we see all things are ready for the marriage of the Lamb. This is the culmination of all things, the event to which all things have been building. This is the eternal union between God and his people, nevermore to be impeded by sin, no more relying on faith and hope because now reality has come. This is the consummation of the betrothal begun when the church was placed in eternal union with Christ before time. The betrothal or covenant was a legally binding promise sworn by God upon his own honour and pictured throughout scripture. Thus Paul writes, 'Husbands love your wives even as Christ loved the church and gave himself for it' (Ephesians 5:25). In this life now we experience the engagement. We have the promise symbolised by the ring, but we have to endure separation and patient anticipation. Then in heaven the marriage will replace the engagement, a marriage of unbroken eternal union. How blessed to be called to that marriage supper (v. 9).

The Lamb's Wife And The Guests

Now the marriage of the Lamb is announced as having come, and the Lamb's wife has made herself ready (vv. 7, 8). The Lamb's wife is the church, triumphant in glory. They are the people whom God the Father elected in Christ before the foundation of the world, the innumerable multitude, the 'much people' of verse 1. In fact, the bride is also every guest at the marriage supper (v. 9) and it is a celebration which lasts eternally. They all share a common faith and are without distinction of rank or fitness to be there (Titus 1:4). The one pointing these things out to John must have appeared in the vision as a glorious being for John falls down to worship him. But he is quickly told to desist for, like John, this glorious creature is simply a fellowservant, one of the brethren who have the testimony of Jesus. All are there on the basis of the faith of Jesus Christ who purchased their redemption from the law's curse by his death at Calvary. This is the spirit of prophecy, the declaration of the truth of the gospel of sovereign grace and particular redemption.

It is traditional for a bride to spend a lot of time, energy and perhaps money on getting herself ready for her wedding. Generally, most brides have helpers to do her hair, apply make-up, and help put the dress on so everything is in its proper place. Everything is geared to creating an impression to draw gasps of admiration from the wedding guests and especially from her husband, the bridegroom. When verse 7 tells us the

Lamb's wife has made herself ready, I do not think it is saying her bridal beauty has anything to do with her own efforts. Rather, as verse 8 tells us, it was granted to her to be arrayed in fine linen. It was a gift granted by grace. She is given a wedding garment, clean and white, composed of the righteousnesses of the saints. Righteousnesses is the word used here, plural righteousness. But it cannot be the works believers do on earth because Isaiah 64:6 says clearly even the best of law-works are filthy rags when viewed in the light of the holiness of God. Indeed, believers establish no personal righteousness by the works of the law, even though we know true faith does produce good works (Galatians 2:21).

What then is this fine linen, this white garment? Whence this saints' righteousnesses that are given to her for a garment? It is the righteousness of God which God's people are made in the Lord Jesus Christ by virtue of his being made their sin and paying the law's penalty for it (2 Corinthians 5:21). It is the righteousness of God imputed to the believer in justification and evidenced by faith. In Romans 4:3-5 we read of Abraham's justification by faith, but be clear, it was not Abraham's believing that was counted to him for righteousness as if his faith was a work traded for righteousness. Rather it was what Abraham believed in, the finished substitutionary redeeming work of Christ. This was made over to him for righteousness. This is the righteousness Christ is made to each of his believing people. You have Christ? You have the righteousness of God. It is righteousness with wisdom, sanctification and redemption, says Paul (1 Corinthians 1:30). Here is righteousness imputed with all the strength of divine legality and a righteous nature imparted by God the Holy Spirit in regeneration. It is the garments of salvation clothing God's people of which Isaiah 61:10 speaks. It is the best robe the father put on the prodigal son in the parable, and without which none will be admitted to the marriage supper of the Lamb (Luke 15:22; Matthew 22:11-13).

What a great blessing it is to be called to this marriage (v. 9). Many are called by a general call as the gospel is preached, but some are effectually called when God the Holy Spirit gives spiritual life in the new birth. This is the greatest blessing of all. 'Blessed is the man whom thou choosest and causest to approach unto thee' (Psalm 65:4). It is God's Spirit who makes his elect people willing in the day of his power to believe the gospel the natural man is sure to reject (Psalm 110:3). Do you have assurance you are among that blessed company? Those called and saved by grace, granted repentance for sin and faith to believe the gospel. This is our marriage union with our glorious God.

The Bridegroom

The marriage is the union of the Lamb and his bride. The Lamb is our great God, the Lord Jesus Christ, in his substitutionary, sacrificial role as his people's sin offering. He is the One by whom alone God and his people can be married for eternity. If you would see God you must behold the Lamb of God. Do not look for Satan's lamb, the False Prophet who deceives multitudes with the signs and wonders of this world (Revelation 13:11). No, the Lamb you must seek is God's Lamb, our Lord Jesus Christ, who saves his people from their sins. Though he is a lion in regal majesty, it is as a Lamb he disarms and defeats Satan.

Though God the Father is hidden from mortal man, in Jesus the Man we are able to behold the Lamb of God (John 1:36) who manifests the unknowable God (John 1:18; 14:9). He laid his glory aside for a little while when he was made of a woman (Galatians 4:4; Philippians 2:5-8; Hebrews 2:9). He was clothed in the likeness of sinful flesh, yet without sin so he might redeem his people. We who believe shall see him in the full glory of God as Jesus prayed to his Father we would (John 17:5). This is the vision John was given of Christ in Revelation 19:11-13. This is the church's bridegroom, glorious but meek and lowly of heart (Matthew 11:29). He is the lover of his people's souls and friend of the redeemed sinner. Verse 7 says, 'let us be glad and rejoice'! Babylon is eternally ended, heaven is attained, the marriage supper is before us.

155

Chapter 23

The Victory Of The Lamb

Revelation 19:11-21

Revelation is not a chronological book. It is seven major visions providing complementary perspectives on the same periods of history, either the time from Christ's ascension to his final return or the whole of created history from the Fall in Eden to the end. At the end of chapter 16 we saw a picture of the end of history but it was not the end of the book. From chapter 17:1 we have seen separate reports of aspects of the end of this world describing the harlot, false religion, Antichrist and the False Prophet. Later, in chapter 20 we will see the end of the devil, Gog and Magog and then in the final sections we will see the new heavens and earth described.

Chapter 17 revealed the truth about false religion, much of it looking like the church of God, and as Christendom regarded as such, even by the unbelieving world. In reality, however, it is found out to be a whore committing spiritual fornication by denying of God's truth. We have seen the historical reality of Antichrist's striving for unified world power in opposition to the justice of God, and in chapter 18 we saw the complete dismantling of every aspect of Babylon, this anti-Christian world with its trade, civilisation, politics, culture and its opposition to the rule of God. But God's people, his church, his elect multitude, though suffering many trials as the consequence of Antichrist's opposition, are taken out of the world before the climax of the end. They are eternally married to Christ and, being united to him, come with him to execute Christ's judgment at Armageddon.

I admit the details and exact steps are difficult to fit together with confidence or certainty but the principles are clear and are clarified by other passages of scripture such as 1 Thessalonians 4:16, 17. Christ will take his people, the dead[20] and the living, out of the world immediately

---

[20] I mean the dead bodies of Christ's people will be taken up in a resurrection condition to be reunited with their spirits which have been with Christ in Paradise since their bodily death.

before the end. The anti-Christian world of Christendom will strive for unity with the peoples of Gog and Magog in a final effort to overthrow the rule of God and this will all end in Armageddon when Christ, united with his church will execute final judgment upon them all.

More About Armageddon

When I first came into contact with what sounded like the gospel at an Arminian Baptist Union church in the north of England, there was much fascination with, and superstition concerning, the Battle of Armageddon. There were one or two 'wise elderly ladies' who seemed to have studied Revelation in depth and had come up with elaborate pictures of what was going to happen. In truth, what they produced and taught as fact was more like Tolkien's 'Lord Of The Rings' than God's word. Their basic mistake was to take everything as literal and chronological rather than seeking to discover the spiritual significance of the graphic symbolism. In their portrayal, things would end with literal horses and literal rivers of blood up to the horses' literal bridles (Revelation 14:17-20).

Taking that approach is like trying to piece together a complex jigsaw puzzle you can never satisfactorily complete. Even if you were to come close to constructing an elaborate picture along these lines it is difficult to see how you could derive beneficial practical application from it for our situation today. Rather, we obtain benefit when we seek to understand the spiritual symbolism as it has unfolded through history. This is seen in both Satan's attempts to produce worldwide unification in opposition to God and his justice, and the vision of final destruction when Christ comes as victor to execute final judgment. The message the Holy Spirit intends God's people to grasp is this: first, this present world will end in crushing judgment; second, Christ will defeat all opposition to his rule; third, God's righteousness and truth will be upheld and executed in strict justice; and, fourth, those, and only those, who are the Lamb's bride with their names written in the Lamb's book of life, will escape in triumph to eternal blessedness in heaven with God.

The Lamb's Bride Again

In the last message we saw the vision of the marriage supper and the Lamb's bride. In Revelation 19:7-10 we noted the clothing of the bride was the gracious qualification for heaven God had accomplished by making them the righteousness of God in Christ. But I want to ask again if you know you are counted among those who constitute Christ's bride. Do you have assurance of salvation from sin? Those with a right to such assurance are marked by three characteristics.

They are brethren who have the testimony of Jesus (v. 10). They believe the gospel not just as a matter of mental assent but as the very basis and core of their lives. They confess with Paul, "for to me to live is Christ". They confess the truth about Jesus of Nazareth being the Christ of God, the promised Messiah of the Old Testament who saves his people from their sins exactly in accordance with the scriptures. They gladly participate in communion, discerning as they do, the body and blood of the Lord Jesus Christ as the sole basis of their justification. They worship God in the Spirit, they rejoice in Christ Jesus as Lord, and they have no confidence in the flesh (Philippians 3:3).

They live in the world but exist in wilderness separation from it. They seek to live at peace with all men and to give no offence other than the offence which the natural man harbours against the gospel. They do not imbibe the culture, values, morals, ambitions and anti-Christian teaching of the world. They live looking for the return of Christ to bring in the unrivalled kingdom of God at the end of time. This is their overriding hope and eternal objective.

I trust these characteristics strike a chord with you and you have assurance of being among those constituting the bride of Christ. When Revelation 19:7 talks of the Lamb's wife having made herself ready, this is what I believe it means.

The Lamb's Victory
In Revelation 19:11-21 we are given a vision of the Lamb's victory. Is this a new vision? I am not sure but it does not really matter whether it is new or part of the sixth vision. The important thing is to see the eternal reality it signifies. Remember again the scene in 2 Kings 6:15-17 with Elisha and his servant surrounded by the forces of Assyria. They obtained heavenly assurance of a far greater company of angels on their side. This is always the way things are in the conflict between Satan and God. We need to remember it when it appears Antichrist is winning. Christ is supreme and we shall see this vision again portray his final triumph over the beast, the False Prophet and all the world powers who serve and worship them. This is another perspective on Armageddon, the final victory of God over Satan. Here we see divine righteousness and justice vindicated, and the lie of Satan eternally crushed.

What are we shown about our King, the captain of our salvation? We are shown symbolism of his supremacy. These pictures are not to be taken literally; for example, how could he literally wear many crowns? How could there be an angel in the literal sun? How could the ravenous birds be literal? Remember Revelation 1:1 where the word signified set

159

the style of the whole book? The visions use the symbolism of literal types to convey the truth of spiritual reality.

Look with me at the symbols given here and see what we can learn. First, John sees in heavenly vision a white horse. This speaks of military triumph; visit any great art gallery and you will find pictures or sculptures of conquering heroes sitting on white stallions. Here the one sat upon this white horse is called 'Faithful and True'. It is God the Son who on earth described himself as The Truth (John 14:6). The vision symbolically pictures the coming reality of Christ judging righteously and making war with all the authority of his supreme office. His name is more than just a label of differentiation from others; it speaks of his character. He is faithful to God the Father, faithful to fulfil the everlasting covenant of salvation of which the entire Godhead made the Son surety. He is faithful to his people in the salvation promises he made to them and he is faithful to his enemies in terms of the just and strict judgment he holds them to. His truth stands in stark contrast to the lies of Satan, the lies you, unbeliever, have believed rather than believing the word of God.

The Son of God came to this earth (Galatians 4:4), laid aside his divine glory and humbled himself to the death of the cross (Philippians 2:5-11). He lived as an outcast, despised and rejected of men without a home to call his own. Before his crucifixion he rode into Jerusalem in humility, not upon a white stallion but on an ass's colt, a scriptural picture of wayward, sinful, fallen man. Now we see him in majesty and certain of victory. Read the first six verses of Psalm 45. It is a glorious picture of Christ, written a thousand years or more before he came to earth. It is the picture we see here in the vision of Revelation 19:11, 12.

In verse 12 we read of his eyes which are able to burn through any barrier to see all hidden secrets. His many crowns are the crowns of defeated usurpers and he has a mysterious name. His name speaks of him as Mediator of the Covenant (Hebrews 12:24) because only he knows fully how his mediation made satisfaction to the offended justice of God for the sins of his elect. God's people believe Christ's mediation for them has accomplished their salvation, we assent gladly to the teaching that Christ's blood paid redemption's price, and we rest in the confident hope of glory this truth gives us. But only Christ knows how his death made full satisfaction for the sins of his Bride.

In verse 13 his clothing is described as 'dipped in blood'. Usually we think of this as his own precious blood shed for his people's redemption at Calvary and I can readily agree with that. But in the context of the passage, this is the Lord judging the world for its sin and exacting what justice demands, namely death. Because the blood is the life, blood must be shed to satisfy the law (Deuteronomy 12:23), either the blood of Christ as the Substitute for his people, or the blood of those judged guilty who have no substitute to stand for them. I think the blood staining of Christ's vesture in this vision is the blood of his enemies as Isaiah 63:2-4 indicates, 'Wherefore art thou red in thine apparel, and thy garments like him that treadeth in the winefat? I have trodden the winepress alone; and of the people there was none with me: for I will tread them in mine anger, and trample them in my fury; and their blood shall be sprinkled upon my garments, and I will stain all my raiment. For the day of vengeance is in mine heart, and the year of my redeemed is come.' This is the blood of rebels shed over generations as the seals are loosed, as the trumpets are sounded and as the vials of wrath are poured out even to the extent of the final wrath at Armageddon. We have seen it already in Revelation 14:20 as a winepress of judgment extracting a 1,600 furlong river of blood to the depth of horse bridles. This is the Lord Jesus Christ, coming to exact just retribution on all rebellion against the rule and law of God and he treads the winepress of the fierceness of the wrath of Almighty God (v. 15).

The Word Of God
If there were any shred of doubt as to who this majestic person riding the white horse is, verse 13 tells us his name is 'The Word Of God'. He is the One who manifests the invisible Godhead to his people (John 1:1, 14, 18; 14:9; Colossians 2:9). The speech proceeding from his mouth is a sharp sword as described in Hebrews 4:12, doing the work of God in conviction of sin; it is the holy scriptures, the Bible, the sword of the Spirit (Ephesians 6:17). Is it any wonder God has given Christ the name which is above every name (Philippians 2:9)? We read in Psalm 138:2 'Thou hast magnified thy word above all thy name.' Do you see how highly exalted the Christ of God is?

Would you see the Father? Would you experience the very essence of the Godhead? Then hear the Son of man speak, "Have I been so long time with you, and yet hast thou not known me, Philip? he that hath seen me hath seen the Father" (John 14:9). This is what it is to preach Christ; this is what the apostles preached, and those to whom they taught the gospel; Jesus the man is the Christ of God (Acts 18:28). This is what John means in his first epistle (1 John 4:1-3) pointing out the benchmark of the truth of God; Jesus the man is the eternal Word of God. He is the One in this vision who smites the nations with his word of judgment. This one majestically riding the white horse is the Son spoken of in Psalm 2 who rules with a rod of iron until everyone is compelled to bow the knee to

Christ either by gospel grace or under the iron rod of justice. I ask you, what will cause you to bow the knee? For certain it is. You will bow to the KING OF KINGS AND LORD OF LORDS (v. 16)

As he rides forth, he is not alone (v. 14). No doubt the armies with him include angels, but also his saints whom he has redeemed. They follow him wherever he goes (Revelation 14:4). Like him they are clothed in white and ride upon white horses giving proof 'that as he is, so are we in this world' (1 John 4:17) and also in the world to come. Note his armies are armed with nothing but his righteousness because, 'the battle is not yours but God's' (2 Chronicles 20:15). This warfare, its weapons and armour, are spiritual, simply the Word of God and prayer.

In verses 17 and 18, ravenous birds are called to come to the feast of flesh the final judgment will bring. Again the language is symbolical and not literal. But what it pictures is very real. In ancient battles, a vivid confirmation of defeat was the vultures feasting on the corpses of the defeated troops; the picture is used many times in scripture concerning God's triumph over his enemies. Look how wide is the scope of those included in the ranks of the defeated; all ranks and classes of people (v. 18), but all with one common trait, they wilfully sinned and despised the justice of God. Their rebellion goes on right to the end as they gather themselves to make war on Christ (v. 19).

However, verses 20 and 21 show us the war they seek to make is over before it has begun. This is the certain end of all opposition to God's rule, righteousness and justice. Is there any escape route? I know of only one. Turn to Revelation 22:16, 17 and see there, in effect, a wide open door of salvation from the destruction of Revelation 19:20, 21. Will you hear the call to come? Or will you try to make the excuse that election stopped you from being on the Lord's side?

Chapter 24

Here And Now And The Final Judgment

Revelation 20

We have been given several perspectives throughout Revelation of the same final judgment and its culmination in what is called in scripture, the Battle of Armageddon. We saw it in chapters 6, 9, 11, 14, 16 and then in the last half of chapter 19. In the last view we saw the final, total victory of Christ and his people over the armies of Satan, the Beast and the False Prophet, all accomplished without a blow other than the sharp sword of the word of his mouth. But now we see a new vision commence in Chapter 20, the seventh vision of the whole book. It spans the period from Christ's ascension to the end of time.

There are numerous books on Revelation, the vast majority of which I reject as delusions from Satan. Nowhere do they go more astray from the truth than in Revelation 20. Often they major on the thousand years of verse 7 and develop absurd and bizarre notions. Differing 'camps' have arisen rallying around opposing schemes of pre- and post-millennial teaching, dividing over whether Christ comes and reigns on earth before or after the literal thousand years of this chapter. Satan loves it because it provides a cunning distraction from the central message of Christ and the effectual salvation he has accomplished. Let us look at Chapter 20 keeping to the principles of interpretation that have guided us so far.

The Angel, The Key, The Chain And The Pit

In earlier visions we saw the power of Satan to deceive in Old Testament times. There was almost universal worship of his beast and the world was infatuated with the delusions of his false prophet. The basis of his deceit was prosperous life and eternal good without the need of satisfaction for God's offended justice. We saw it begin with Babel in Genesis 11 as Satan attempted to unify the then world in opposition to the rule of God. But, of course, God frustrated his purposes as he has done ever since.

163

Before Christ came in time and redeemed the people of his choice, Satan stirred up five great empires in opposition to the symbolical people of God, Israel. We read of these in the book of Daniel. These empires were his various attempts to achieve worldwide dominion through unity in opposition to the truth of God. Egypt, Assyria, Chaldea (Babylonia), Medo-Persia and Greece all employed force of arms to subdue opposition and unite the peoples of the known world in common cultures and idolatrous philosophies. Each one of them went a long way to achieving Satan's objective but ultimately they all failed. Then, after Greece, the Roman empire, the iron legs with feet of iron and clay of Nebuchadnezzar's dream (Daniel 2:33), was raised up in great strength. That empire brought the best roads there had ever been, it brought civilisation to barbarians, a system of justice and the rule of law albeit greatly abused at times. But just like all the others, as widely as it spread, it came nowhere near subduing the entire world as Satan had intended.

Throughout this Old Testament period, there had been war in heaven between Michael and his angels and Satan and his demons (Revelation 12:7) over the legitimacy of the Old Testament saints who had died being in heaven. Satan's claim was they were sinners and rightfully his, and their being in heaven violated God's justice, which Satan despised anyway. Michael countered that the Lamb slain from the foundation of the world (Revelation 13:8) procured redemption for them. But Satan objected that in the space-time creation no satisfaction had thus far been made for sin.

With such immense power granted to him, we might ask why Satan did not win the argument. The answer loud and clear from scripture is the blood of the Lamb overcame him (Revelation 12:11). From the moment Christ came and died the death of the cross for his people's sin, Satan knew his time was limited (Revelation 12:12). The Lord Jesus rose from the dead, vindicated his substitutionary sacrifice, and ascended to heavenly glory. Now we see Satan's powers further limited.

In verses 1 to 3 of chapter 20 we see the empowered messenger of God coming to the realm where Satan prowls seeking whom he may destroy (1 Peter 5:8). The way he destroys is by perpetuating his lie to Eve in Eden, 'Has God really said ... ?' He deceived Adam and deceives the progeny of Adam to follow him in doubting and disbelieving God. Throughout Old Testament days the vast majority of humankind fell for his lie, the exceptions being the line God preserved in Israel from which Messiah would come, and even then as Romans 9:6 puts it, 'they are not all Israel which are of Israel'. Looking at history before Christ came, it appears that Satan had more or less free rein.

But now we see in this seventh vision of Revelation, God's empowered messenger come into Satan's realm with a key and a chain. These are symbols of restraint. When I was a young man with a young family I struggled financially to run a family car. I kept a series of 'old bangers' running by do-it-yourself maintenance often requiring a visit to a local car breaker's yard for second-hand parts. This particular yard was a very unpleasant environment and central to its security was a fierce German Shepherd dog chained to a large wooden kennel from which the yard owner released it at night to patrol the locked compound. The search for a needed car part often involved walking close to the dog which was terrifying. However, you were safe as long as you stayed beyond the length of its chain. The dog could only go as far as the chain would allow. That is the picture of this vision of Satan being restrained in his deception of the world.

The key the angel has in his hand is the key of the bottomless pit we saw in an earlier vision. In Revelation 9:1 Satan was given the key to release a plague of demonic locusts. The bottomless pit is the temporary abode of the devil and his demons. We read in 2 Peter 2:4, 'God spared not the angels that sinned, but cast them down to hell, and delivered them into chains of darkness, to be reserved unto judgment.' But note the key is God's to give and take back according to his sovereign will. The chain likewise is God's to determine its length. The power is God's to give to his angel to restrain Satan as much as he ordains.

What then is the nature and extent of this restraint? It is a binding, imprisoning and setting of an unbreakable seal. Its purpose is that Satan should deceive the nations no more as he had done with the empires before Christ came to accomplish redemption for his elect. What was the nature of the deceit? He deceived them concerning divine righteousness and justice, and the salvation of God's people, as he had done throughout Old Testament times. Which nations has he been deceiving and is now not able to deceive? Look down to verse 8; the nations of Gog and Magog in the four quarters of the earth are those he is restrained from deceiving. He is no longer able to unite them in worldwide opposition against the people and kingdom of God. Ezekiel 38 and 39 sheds light on this difficult idea. There the nations of Gog and Magog come in force against greater Israel, but remember from the measuring of the temple in Revelation 11 that only the core of the temple in Jerusalem represents the true Israel of God. The outer court, the city and the rest of the land represented mere Christendom which in truth is anti-Christian. When we read the Old Testament and see the repeated idolatry and unfaithfulness of 'greater Israel' it is clear that Satan's deceiving of the nations had

165

almost subsumed even the symbolical (albeit idolatrous) people of God into worldwide union with Satan's empires and only a godly remnant was preserved from which Christ would come according to the flesh (Romans 1:3). After Christ came and accomplished redemption for his people, Satan in his great wrath (Revelation 12:12) wanted to continue his deception of the nations in uniting world power against God's people, but he is restrained and prevented from having his way for 1,000 years.

The Thousand Years
What is the significance of the 1,000 years? Is it a literal 1,000 years or is it symbolical of something else? Remember we must be careful not to mix literal and symbolical language in the same vision. It is clear the key, the chain and the pit are symbolical so why should the 1,000 years not be symbolical also? The number 10 symbolises completeness, worldly perfection, in contrast to the seven of divine perfection. There are ten commandments, ten plagues in Egypt, ten virgins in the parable, ten talents given to the servants and more Biblical examples. It is a fulness as determined by God, so 1,000 is ten cubed. 1,000 years represents a long time, a time that is complete for God's purposes, but also a distinctly limited time.

In Old Testament times the nations of Gog and Magog repeatedly attacked Israel in Satan's attempt to destroy the Seed of the woman which was Christ. In New Testament times those nations are relatively quiet in world history. Most activity appears focused in the nations of Christendom, the spiritual whore. The reason for this is clear. In New Testament times, Satan is restrained in his ability to deceive Gog and Magog as he did in Old Testament times. Since Satan has been restrained in this 1,000 year symbolical period, Christendom has actually spread and prospered, like greater Israel did at times in the Old Testament, and in some places even the symbolical temple court, the inner core of it, has flourished. The gospel and its influence have spread widely through the world and there have been pockets of true believers in many places, including among in the nations of Gog and Magog.

In the United kingdom, think of the time when Whitefield was preaching, when Gadsby, Huntington, Hawker, Warburton, Philpot, Spurgeon and many more ministered in our land. There were thriving assemblies of true saints with faithful ministers boldly declaring the true gospel. These were found widely throughout this country and further afield. How different to the situation today. What has brought about the change? I would suggest the symbolical 1,000 years has ended and Satan's restraint has been loosed as we shall see shortly. How long was the period of his restraint literally? We cannot be sure but it seems to me that it was from the time of Christ's ascension until about 30 or 40 years ago. Look at the pace of change and the degree of degeneration that has occurred in that time in many once-faithful churches.

Meanwhile In Heaven
Verse 4 describes the situation in heaven during the time of the thousand years of restraint of Satan. The souls of the saints who have died on the earth are consciously reigning with Christ in heaven. These are true believers, the elect of God, justified sinners. They are in themselves no better than anyone else but have been called by God's grace and made willing in the day of his power to follow Christ. They were marked out in their earthly life by not bearing the mark of the beast, by not worshipping his image along with the rest of the world; they were marked with the seal of God's Spirit (Revelation 7:3). Fellowship with Christ is their continuing experience after physical death, for, to be absent from the body for a believer is to be present with the Lord (2 Corinthians 5:8); there is no purgatory in the purposes of God. As Jesus said to the penitent thief on the cross next to him, 'This day you shall be with me in Paradise'.

In verse 5 we read of the state of 'death limbo' in which unbelievers who die remain until the 1,000 years are completed. In contrast, in verse 6 we read of the blessedness of God's saints who have risen straight from death into the conscious experience of the glory of heaven, and upon whom the second death of final judgment has no power. They are reigning as kings and serving as priests of God and of Christ.

Loosed For A Little Season
Verse 3 states clearly the restraint of Satan will come to an end and verse 7 confirms at the end of the 1,000 years he is released to deceive Gog and Magog once more in preparation for battle. The picture of verse 9 appears to me to be very close to what the true church of Christ is experiencing today. The world as represented by Gog and Magog is encompassing the camp of the saints and the beloved city. Zion is that city, the true church of Christ. Recall Ezekiel 38 and 39 and its picture of the godless, anti-Christ world battling against the righteousness of God. There seems to be no national borders any more (Revelation 9:14; 16:12) and even the superficially moral culture of Christendom has been choked by the godless influence of Gog and Magog overturning national laws based on Biblical principles, especially in recent decades.

I am aware that many will object to these ideas. Some may even label me racist for writing such things; nothing could be further from the truth.

167

I have true brethren in the true faith whose ethnicity is utterly irrelevant to our bonds of unity in Christ. The innumerable multitude that John saw was completely ethnically mixed, for God so loved the world, not just the Jews (John 3:16). There are true Christian churches located in the midst of the symbolical nations of Gog and Magog. But also I am aware it would be easy to point to seeming inconsistencies in this analysis of the text where sometimes Antichrist is Christendom, and other times Gog and Magog overruns Christendom. But try to see the overriding principles of the picture. Satan has been loosed from his 1,000 year restraint and the true church of Christ, not the whore of Christendom, appears to be lying dead in the streets (Revelation 11:8) at least as far as being viable, functioning fellowships is concerned. Of course, I may be wrong, but does anyone have a better explanation of the phenomenal, and accelerating changes in world politics, economics, philosophy, culture and freedom of movement of the last 50 years?

Let me ask you, believer, do these days frighten you? Remember it is described as but a little season. It will soon be finished, and fire from God will devour all of your enemies. The devil will be cast into the lake of fire without trial for there will be no need to determine his guilt.

The Throne And Two Books
There is only one return of Christ but there is an order within it. The dead saints, living saints, and then all the rest of mankind will be raised for judgment. For those saints who have died this will be the second resurrection uniting their glorified souls with new, heavenly bodies. The details are the subject of another study but you can read it for yourself in 1 Corinthians 15 and in 1 Thessalonians 4.

Here, at the end of Revelation 20, we see in a vision everyone who has ever lived, without exception, assembled before God's throne of judgment at the end of time. Do not trip over any trivial stumbling-block such as the improbable logistics of arranging such an event; this is symbolical and takes place in the spiritual realm, not the physical. The truth and certainty of it is well established in scripture. For example, 2 Corinthians 5:10 and Romans 14:10 agree we must all stand before the judgment seat of Christ, and Hebrews 9:27 confirms the appointment with death for all and after death the judgment. The judgment is a measuring; when you need to be sure of the length of something you measure it against an objective standard, a tape measure. The objective standard of judgment is what verse 12 calls, the books.

In an English court of law, a person's deeds are measured against the standard of the law defined in the law books. In the final judgment of heaven, the works of men and women which are recorded faithfully in the books are measured against the standard of God's law, his righteousness. In verse 14, death and hell were cast into the lake of fire, that is, as verse 13 makes clear, those death and hell gave up to the judgment are cast into the lake of fire. Verse 15 completes the horrendous symbolism; horrendous because sin is horrendous in the judgment of God. So all are judged in accordance with the records of the books. But there is a very significant exception here.

There is another book opened. It is the Lamb's book of life. It contains the names of all of God's elect, chosen in Christ before the foundation of the world. These, too, are sinners, every one of them, but sinners redeemed from the curse of the law by the death and shed blood of Jesus Christ their Surety and Substitute. The justice-satisfying vengeance that falls on all sinners in the final judgment has already fallen on the Christ of God. Therefore, it is deemed to have fallen also upon the people placed 'in him', that is, in eternal union with him before the beginning of time. The final judgment finds no debt outstanding against any of the names written in the Lamb's book of life. This accords with what Jeremiah was inspired to write long before Christ came to earth. He wrote, 'In those days, and in that time, saith the Lord, the iniquity of Israel shall be sought for, and there shall be none; and the sins of Judah, and they shall not be found: for I will pardon them whom I reserve' (Jeremiah 50:20). The books recording the works of mankind hold no record of any sin against the names in the Lamb's book of life. Consequently, no one is able to bring any charge worthy of death against them for the simple reason Christ has already died in their place (Romans 8:33, 34). Is it any wonder that Revelation 13:8 calls him the Lamb slain from the foundation of the world? Anyone trusting in Christ is in eternal union with him, and standing where they do, the fire of the wrath of God against sin has already fallen; the ground is already scorched and can burn no more.

Here is the most important question you can ever ask yourself. Is my name written in the Lamb's book of life? How can I be sure I am among the elect of God? Peter says we can be sure through faith, and in following Christ (2 Peter 1:10); does that sound too arduous for one of weak, sinful flesh? Jesus said 'come unto me all ye that labour and are heavy laden and I will give you ... rest for your souls' (Matthew 11:28).

Chapter 25

'All things new'

Revelation 21:1-8

We are coming to the climax of the seventh vision and the end of the book of Revelation. John is shown the conclusion of this sin-cursed space-time creation and its complete renewal. He is shown the completed purposes of God in electing grace come to its fulfilment and Christ's redeemed people in a state of eternal bliss. Think of those who were our brethren and sisters in Christ here until they died; they are in that state now. I heard recently of a dear brother, serving Christ in Mexico, being suddenly taken to glory though not yet 60 years old. As I write, he is seeing and experiencing the reality of the things of which John writes. Do you believe that?

Let me remind you once again of the seven perspectives or visions of created time that we have seen. Created time is what constitutes history and it truly is Christ's story. First we saw Christ in the midst of his church in the world throughout the period from his ascension to his return. Second, we saw Christ opening God's seven-sealed plan for the defeat of Satanic rebellion and the salvation of his elect. The third vision showed Christ executing seven trumpets of providential judgment, frustrating Satan's Antichrist ambitions. The fourth revealed Christ's church, his redeemed people from Genesis 3:21 to his second coming at the end of time, bringing forth Christ according to the flesh for the purpose of redemption, all the while suffering Satanic persecution by the beast and the false prophet. Then fifth, we saw the seven vials of divine wrath poured out. Sixth, was the exposure and final destruction of Babylon, the beast and the false prophet and now, seventh, we are given to understand history since Christ's ascension leading up to the final judgment and the glory of the New Jerusalem.

Revelation 20 showed us the period from Christ's ascension to the end, with Satan restrained for a symbolical 1,000 years from deceiving Gog and Magog as he had before, and that is why he still has not succeeded in his objectives. Then he is released for a little season and we

171

saw close parallels between the days we are living in now and the description of that time. But it is soon brought to an end and fire comes down from heaven; the devil is cast into the lake of fire along with all whose names are not found written in the Lamb's book of life.

The End

Isaiah 34:4 states that God will bring this sin-cursed creation to an end as easily as a scroll of paper is rolled up. This is confirmed by 2 Peter 3:10 and Revelation 6:14. Unbelievers scoff at the idea, thinking things will continue as they always have (2 Peter 3:4), just as they did in the days of Noah before the flood came and swept them all away. All such say to God, 'Depart from us, for we desire not the knowledge of thy ways. What is the Almighty that we should serve him? And what profit have we if we pray to him?' (Job 21:14, 15). For them the only prospect is the eternity of hell, but for those whose names are written in the Lamb's book of life, there is a new heaven and a new earth (Revelation 21:1).

A New Creation

In Revelation 21:1 John sees in a vision a new creation. No trace is left of the old creation, the current one in which we live. There is no more sea and if you are still thinking literally you might well be disappointed by that as I would be because here one of my favourite activities is walking the coastal paths of Cornwall and enjoying the beautiful blue sea. Remember this is a vision of spiritual reality; the sea is symbolical in Revelation and the lack of it is similarly symbolical. The sea in previous visions has symbolised the turmoil of humanity (Revelation 17:15); it was from the sea the beast emerged, a sea of worldly opposition to the things of God. The sea is also a symbol of separation, not so keenly felt in these days of jet travel but how separating it must have felt to previous generations where the sea stood as a dangerous and arduous barrier to separated peoples. In the new creation there will be nothing to separate saints and angels from one another and their glorious God. This is the new heavens and earth in which dwells righteousness (2 Peter 3:13). Well before Christ came, Isaiah was inspired by God's Spirit to write 'For, behold, I create new heavens and a new earth: and the former shall not be remembered, nor come into mind. But be ye glad and rejoice for ever in that which I create: for, behold, I create Jerusalem a rejoicing, and her people a joy' (Isaiah 65:17, 18). Paul tells us in Romans 8:22 that the whole creation has been groaning with longing to be delivered from the bondage of corruption resulting from sin. Well, here it is accomplished in this final vision.

172

A New Jerusalem

Remember, this is a vision. This holy city (v. 2) is the church triumphant, the redeemed people of God, Christ's bride as we have seen already in an earlier vision. Psalm 48:1, 2 speaks of Zion of which Old Testament, physical Jerusalem, only at times, was but a pale shadow. In Galatians 4:25, 26, Paul compares physical Jerusalem with what is above, the new Jerusalem of this vision; the former is in bondage with all her children but the new Jerusalem is free. This is the city of Hebrews 11:10, a city which has foundations whose builder and maker is God. This is Mount Sion, the city of the living God, the heavenly Jerusalem (Hebrews 12:22).

A city, in the mind of the first century people, has walls to protect its people from attack; it is symbolical of a place of permanent residence with many people, with mutual security and safety. But the city John sees in the vision is also a bride made ready for her husband, adorned with righteousness in election, redemption and regeneration. She is coming from her Father's house out of heaven, as Jude says 'the Lord cometh with ten thousand of his saints' (Jude 14), coming to be permanently united with the Son of God, as was said by him, 'Behold I and the children which God hath given me' (Isaiah 8:18; Hebrews 2:13).

With God For Ever

The believer's experience of God now on earth is fleeting and always marred by sin. God makes his abode with the believer but his presence is not always felt. In New Jerusalem the fellowship will be uninterrupted (v. 3). There will be permanent, perfect communion unaffected by sin. This is beyond the capability of our mortal understanding as John wrote in 1 John 3:2, 'Beloved, now we are the sons of God, and it doth not yet appear what we shall be: but we know that, when he shall appear, we shall be like him; for we shall see him as he is.'

Eternal Bliss

With sin gone, all cause of pain and sorrow will be removed (v. 4). Former things, the things of this mortal life, will have passed away. The patriarchs saw it by faith and longed for it (Hebrews 11). Anyone feeling the curse of sin, the justice of condemnation and the blessedness of redemption has a good hope of attaining to it. There is no purgatory, that is a Roman Catholic error of post-death second chance through works. There are no degrees of reward for the works of believers in this life. There will be no sorrow over the lost, as hard as that might seem now, because in heaven there shall be no more sorrow or tears. There will be no looking back as Lot's wife looked back to Sodom. No, there will be nothing but everlasting joy and glory in the intimate presence of God.

Promised By God

John hears the sovereign God speaking from the throne of glory (v. 5). He who said in the beginning, let there be light and there was light, has said, behold I make all things new. Does it sound too good to be true? You have God's solemn word of truth that everything that John saw is true and faithful. He who has spoken from the throne of supreme power has decreed it and it cannot but come to fruition.

As Good As Already Done

It is done (v. 6). In eternity, outside of time it is already done. There is no possibility of it not being the experience of every child of God. The eternal God has spoken, he who is Alpha and Omega, the first and the last, the author and finisher of our faith, the creator and judge of all. He has spoken and not a word of God fails because as we learn from 2 Corinthians 5:18, 'all things are of God'.

The Great Divide

Let us bring this right up close. Does this matter to you and me? Is Revelation just a piece of fascinating literature that leaves you the option, however impressed you might have been by aspects of it, to shrug your shoulders and set it aside for another time, perhaps when death might seem to be a closer prospect? How foolish to think that.

A universal divide is coming (vv. 6-8). Our Lord in his earthly ministry, in the days before he went to the cross, spoke of this divide, 'When the Son of man shall come in his glory, and all the holy angels with him, then shall he sit upon the throne of his glory: And before him shall be gathered all nations: and he shall separate them one from another, as a shepherd divideth his sheep from the goats: And he shall set the sheep on his right hand, but the goats on the left. Then shall the King say unto them on his right hand, Come, ye blessed of my Father, inherit the kingdom prepared for you from the foundation of the world: ... Then shall he say also unto them on the left hand, Depart from me, ye cursed, into everlasting fire, prepared for the devil and his angels' (Matthew 25:31-34, 41). Here, in Revelation 21, right in the middle of faithful and true words about the bliss of heaven is a stark warning not to complacently presume on God's mercy.

Those who inherit all the glory of heaven are thirsty now for the things of God. They long to know him, to spend eternity in his presence, to be clothed with his righteousness, to enjoy perpetual, timeless communion. They are believers; they trust Christ and seek to do his will, and we read, they overcome, overcome by faith all the opposition of Satan and the world. This faith is symbolised by the fountain of the water of life freely given by God. Despite many failures and falls they keep coming back to Christ, 'looking unto Jesus the author and finisher of their faith'.

The water God gives is spiritual water to quench spiritual thirst (Matthew 5:6), the water of life, as Jesus promised, 'If any man thirst, let him come unto me, and drink. He that believeth on me, as the scripture hath said, out of his belly shall flow rivers of living water (John 7:37, 38). They shall inherit all things, all that is Christ's and to which he is heir, for his people are joint heirs with him. The thirsting sinners of whom these verses speak, who by fleshly nature are children of wrath even as others, have become inheritors of every privilege of being sons of God.

But, now again, there is a great contrast (v. 8). The 'fearful' suggests those who profess Christianity but are ashamed of God's gospel, who fear worldly opposition and isolation, who ultimately and enduringly are unfaithful to Christ because whatever they might outwardly profess, they are, in fact, unbelieving. All manner of sins are added to the list of all who reject the gospel of Christ, who have lived according to the call of Satan and his kingdom. As we saw earlier, they all have as their philosophy concerning God the words of Job, 'Depart from us, for we desire not the knowledge of thy ways. What is the Almighty that we should serve him? And what profit have we if we pray to him?' (Job 21:14, 15). Is that where you stand concerning God, his Christ and the gospel of his grace to sinners? If it is, then heed the warning of verse 8. Your short life will soon end in death and after that the judgment and hell, not the heaven of God. But look again at Revelation 22:17 and hear the gracious call while for you there is yet time.

Chapter 26

God's Eternal Paradise

Revelation 21:9-22:5

Having shown us the end of this world, the destruction of Babylon, signifying all false religion, the final judgment of all sin and rebellion against the rule of God, the confinement of Satan and all who bear his mark in hell, John saw the New Jerusalem, the new heavens and new earth. In the passage before us now, he is shown more detail.

The end is coming and there are good reasons to believe we are presently living in Satan's little season (Revelation 20:3). Believers need to watch and be ready, to seek first the kingdom of God and his righteousness, to lay up treasure in heaven and to look for that eternal city which also is certainly coming and is even now the experience of saints who have died believing in Christ.

In contrast, if this life is all there is then go ahead and strive to get whatever you can out of it. As Paul told the Corinthians, 'if in this life only we have hope in Christ, we are of all men most miserable' (1 Corinthians 15:19). But this life is not all there is! What is the point of living for God? Psalm 19:11 says in keeping God's word there is great reward. The service and enjoyment of God for eternity is, as the catechumen knows, 'the chief end of man'. God promised Abraham, when he was still called Abram, great blessings. He said, "Fear not Abram: I am thy shield and thy exceeding great reward" (Genesis 15:1). Do we have any idea as believers how great is our eternal reward? Sin mars everything in this life. Paul wrote, 'Eye hath not seen, nor ear heard, neither have entered into the heart of man, the things which God hath prepared for them that love him. But God hath revealed them unto us by his Spirit' (1 Corinthians 2:9, 10). Here in Revelation 21 and 22 in vision and spiritual metaphor, in symbolism of physically impossible pictures, the great truth of God's eternal Paradise is unveiled.

A Bride That Is A City

In Revelation 21:9 one of the destroying angels who swept away the old creation at the end of time now shows John more of the new creation, and the bride of Christ. This bride is the Lamb's wife. The Lamb is God, specifically the Christ of God, seen in his eternal condition as the one slain for the justification of his people, his bride and his church. We read something of this bride in Ephesians 5:25-27, 32. Human marriage at its very best is a dim picture of this eternal marriage of the Lamb and his church. The bride is the elect people of God, chosen in Christ before time began (Ephesians 1:4; 2 Timothy 1:9). Into time he came to redeem them from the curse of the law by being made a curse for them when he bore their sins in his own body on the tree (Galatians 3:13; 1 Peter 2:24).

But you need a vantage point to see this bride (v. 10) the reason being that the bride is a great city, holy Jerusalem, the Jerusalem which is above (Galatians 4:26). She comes down from God having the glory of God (v. 11). And what strikes John powerfully in the vision of the bride and city, is her pure light. Throughout scripture, the light of God always stands in contrast to the darkness of Satan.

The City's Dimensions

Now we read the dimensions of holy Jerusalem (vv. 12-17). If we found a city planner could we ask them to draw what John saw? No. It is a vision. Rather, the question to ask is, what ideas does the vision convey?

The first thing to note is it is huge; it is a cube with sides of length 12,000 furlongs or 1,500 miles. It has a 220ft high wall with twelve gates and twelve foundations named with the names of the Apostles. How can a three dimensional cube have a two dimensional surrounding wall? This is clearly not possible in terms of this space-time creation, so what does it picture?

The wall speaks of completion. Nehemiah's work after the Babylonian captivity involved rebuilding and completing the broken walls of Jerusalem for defence against the enemies of God. Walls in scripture are associated with salvation; Isaiah, speaking of a heavenly vision of Zion says, "thou shalt call thy walls Salvation, and thy gates Praise" (Isaiah 60:18).

The cube of the city alludes to the tabernacle's Holy of Holies where dwelt the presence of God with his people, and Revelation 21:3 reminded us of God's promise to dwell with his people. But why such a large cube? Keep hold of the idea this is the language and symbolism of vision; the size speaks of the great multitude which no man can number. We keep hearing the number 12. That is 3x4, the number of God 'working on' the

178

number of creation which symbolises the election of grace; hence there are 12 tribes of Israel, or patriarchs and 12 Apostles of the New Testament making 24 elders in heaven in total. There are 12 gates with 12 angels who gather in the harvest of God's redeemed people, and there are 12 foundations in the wall which speaks of the Apostles, whose doctrine, fellowship, breaking of bread and prayers formed the basis of New Testament church faith and practice (Acts 2:42). Ten speaks of completeness or fulness and when it is squared or cubed and combined with the 'twelves' we get a number which is very particular to God but innumerable even to the redeemed saints.

The 'symbolical geometry' of the city, the Lamb's wife, portrays in the language of this creation, the mysteries of the new one. It underlines the completion of God's work of salvation, his particular redemption of the people he chose in Christ before the foundation of the world and their eternal presence with God in intimate fellowship and communion. We do not see clearly what we shall be, as John wrote in his first epistle, but we who believe shall be with Christ and we shall be like him.

Materials
In verses 18 to 21 we have a description of the materials of the city's construction. Remember this is symbolical not literal. That is one feature that distinguishes the truth of God's word from the falsehood of, for example, Islam. The 'heaven' of Islam is couched in very physical and literal terms; Islamic men are deluded into thinking when they die as martyrs in the cause of their god they are rewarded in heaven with literally 70 virgins for sexual pleasure. What utterly carnal and abusively exploitative thinking! No, the true heaven of the true God is not of this world but spiritual. When we read of precious earthly materials we do not covet ownership of jewels but the spiritual riches they symbolise.

We read of gold, multi-coloured precious stones and pearls. Their appearance is of purity, clarity, rarity and great value. They are precious materials, enthralling to look at. If you have visited the Tower of London and paid the extra to see the crown jewels you will have been awe-struck with their priceless beauty, yet they come nowhere near the reverence of John's vision of the holy city.

Gold speaks of faith (1 Peter 1:7); only those who have the true faith of Christ, the gift of God, will enter this eternal city. Jewels speak of shining light and pearls indicate the one pearl of great price (Matthew 13:46) the gospel of Christ and the Christ of the gospel, and in verse 21, each gate being a pearl speaks of the only entrance being by the door who is Christ (John 10:9).

179

The Temple

In verses 22 to 27 we learn that the only temple in the city is 'The Lord God Almighty and the Lamb'. In the Old Testament, the tabernacle and then the temple in Jerusalem was where God dwelt on earth symbolically with his people. It was a small part of Jerusalem in a much larger country of Israel. As a Jew, the temple in Jerusalem was where you had to go to be close to the presence of God, but even there, the way into the holiest of all was barred to all but the High Priest, and then only once a year on the Day of Atonement. Then he ventured in with the blood of an acceptable sacrifice, a sacrifice picturing and pointing to the sacrifice of Christ (1 Corinthians 5:7). It was a time of great nervousness as to whether the High Priest would be accepted or whether he would be struck dead for daring to enter inappropriately.

But in the New Jerusalem, all is the temple; the whole of it is the eternal presence of God with his people in perfect, sinless fellowship (Revelation 21:3). It is all the Holy of Holies and all God's people have free access because Christ has gone before them with his own precious blood as the acceptable sacrifice for them all. Just as God is the Temple of the New Jerusalem and the New Jerusalem is all Temple, so God is its perpetual, spiritual, light. As believers now on earth we see the light of the knowledge of the glory of God in the face of Jesus Christ (2 Corinthians 4:6), so in heaven he is all the light and all we need.

In verse 24 we see the nations of them which are saved walking in God's light; these are the redeemed from every nation and they are engaged in constant activity, neither bored nor fatigued. They are kings of the earth, who were sinners on earth but made kings and priest unto God (Revelation 1:6; 5:10). The glory and honour of the nations must be the glory of God (v. 26) with which he endows his redeemed people when he clothes them with the seamless robe of his righteousness. And this eternal city will be glorious in its freedom from all defilement (v. 27); there shall be no sin, no idolatry, no spiritual adultery in vivid contrast to the defilement of Babylon.

Paradise

The first five verses of chapter 22 picture the Paradise of God; the language has echoes of the Garden of Eden before the Fall. It has a river which symbolises the constant source of life-giving spiritual water from God. It has the Tree of Life (v. 2) echoing the one in Eden that Adam needed for daily sustenance, but here it pictures unending communion with God. Note however, unlike Eden, there is no tree of the knowledge

180

of good and evil in this vision of heaven for there is no probation there. Unlike Adam in Eden, God's glorified saints will be incapable of sinning. The fruit and leaves of the Tree of Life indicate a perpetual harvest and a perpetual cure from the sin left behind in this creation.

It all speaks of the life and blessedness of the glorified church in heaven but described in the imagery of the Garden of Eden, the Paradise of God. Because there is no sin there, there is no more curse, just the royal presence of God and the Lamb. All God's saved people shall be engaged in perpetual, delightful service with the face of Christ ever in their sight (2 Corinthians 4:6). Here is a picture of bliss. All those branded with the name of God, not the mark of the beast, living perpetually in perfect spiritual light, serving God and reigning over God's new heaven and earth for ever.

Do I understand it? Can I accurately picture it and describe it? Not at all, at least not with the language of this world, but it sounds wonderful beyond imagination just the same. It is the promise of God for the people he has saved from their sins.

Conclusion
This is the culmination of all of God's eternal purpose of grace. This is his Kingdom come to its ultimate fulfilment, the bliss to which his servants on earth look and hope, and for which he taught his disciples to pray. As believers, if we are true to the gospel, we hold everything in this life lightly, on open not grasping palms. We enjoy the good, we employ the gifts, but we know they will all soon be gone and replaced with that which is far better. While we remain here we seek to do all as unto the Lord and we wait and watch for his imminent return.

What we have seen represents an eternal marriage supper to which the gospel of redeeming blood has bidden us to come. Have you ever felt the rejection of hearing of a party to which you were not invited? Well, listen carefully because there is an invitation in verse 17 and I see nothing to suggest it is not directed to you who thirst for peace with God in his eternal Paradise.

The Kingdom Of God Triumphant

Chapter 27

'Behold, I come quickly …'

Revelation 22:6-21

The mark of a good book is the extent to which it affects you; your thinking, opinions, behaviour and attitude to others. Has the book of Revelation changed you? It has told us things that must happen in this space-time creation before God's kingdom comes to perfect fulfilment and unrivalled permanence.

Through seven distinct visions we have seen differing perspectives on the same history of this world and God's control of all things. The visions have shown us God's utter intolerance of sin and of the kingdom of Satan. Satan acquired this kingdom in a bloodless coup d'état when Adam, in the Fall in the garden of Eden, surrendered to Satan the rule over creation God had delegated to him. Revelation has shown us God's plan for the overthrow of Satan's rebellion and the triumph of God's kingdom of righteousness and peace. We have seen Christ in his church in the world, from the time of his ascension to his final return, keeping his people from the destruction Satan desires. We have seen Christ uniquely qualified to open the seals of God's plan for restoration of his kingdom, we have seen the trumpets and vials of intensifying judgment and wrath pour from God on Satan's kingdom. We have, I trust, better understood history, seeing it as the outworking of Satan's Antichrist despite the 1,000 year restraint on his ambitions for worldwide unity in opposition to God's kingdom. We have seen very recent history to be closely connected with the little season in which Satan is loosed from his restraint. We saw Babylon for what it really has always been, its destruction and the final judgment, and we saw the new heavens and earth of God's eternal kingdom in which dwells perpetual righteousness.

Have you been spoken to by this book, or has it left you unmoved? My prayer is it has moved you to take seriously the brevity and fragility of your life and to view the sheer vanity of the world and its dark spiritual

183

destiny. To do as Bunyan's Pilgrim and flee from the City of Destruction obtaining by faith a good hope of reaching the Celestial City. Well, here in the last verses of Revelation, in the passage before us now, is the conclusion of the whole matter. Here we have sixteen verses of epilogue with no new vision, but we do see the affirmation of key things.

Affirming The Truth Of God
In verse 6, the angel speaking to John affirms the truth and faithfulness of these sayings. Which sayings does he mean? This is the last chapter of the Bible as it has been providentially preserved for God's people in this world. I am convinced the angel means more than just the words of Revelation and he means the whole Bible. Look at verses 18 and 19 at the end of the whole Bible, where a stern warning is given by the speaker, the Lord Jesus Christ (v. 16). He who is the very Word of God, cautions us not to add to or take away from anything written in the words of the prophecy of this book. He means the whole Bible; a similar warning is given in Deuteronomy 4:2 in the last book of Moses. Then at the end of the Old Testament in Malachi 4:4, God's people are called upon to remember the law of Moses. It all reinforces the idea that the Bible is God's total Revelation of his truth to us; he has exalted it above all his name (Psalm 138:2).

In verses 7, 12, 13, 16 and 18, the 'I' who speaks is God manifested in Christ who is the Word of God (John 1:1). He is Almighty God who is Jesus the Deliverer and Saviour. He is the Root of David and David's offspring according to the flesh. He came to save his people from their sins (Matthew 1:21). He cannot lie, his word is true and it is faithful. You can rely on it to happen as he has said. The Word's revelations must shortly be fulfilled. The Lord Jesus Christ speaks now through the written word, by his ministry gifts to his church, that is, his Spirit-anointed preachers so his sheep might hear the Good Shepherd's voice and follow him (John 10:27).

In this fallen world of shallow falsehood and fickle superstition, will you hear the truth testified by God and believe it must happen shortly? Ask yourself, from all we have seen in the visions of Revelation, how much has already been shown to be true and how little remains to happen before the end?

Reaffirming The Coming Of God
We all, in our natural, sinful state of unbelief listen overmuch to Satan's lie concerning the truth of God. 'Has God really said ... ?' (Genesis 3:1-5). We tend to doubt God's testimony concerning the return of the Lord

Jesus Christ in judgment. Yet, his return is the culmination of history and throughout Revelation the fact of his return has been repeated and emphasised. Here in chapter 20 Christ himself asserts it in verses 7, 12 and 20. Will you believe him? Revelation has described the history of the world with amazing accuracy, and foretold the last 1,900 years of it before it happened; why should it not also be true about Christ's return?

The end of all things is fast approaching. Ask yourself whether you are conscious of that fact, whether you are looking for it expectantly, even hoping for it. Are you with those in verse 20 who say, "even so, come, Lord Jesus"? Or are you like those in the parable of the supper (Luke 14:16-24) who made excuses not to attend?

Confirming The Eternal Judgment Of God

If Christ's return in final judgment is certain and imminent, heed the warning. You cannot sit on the fence about it. Verse 11 tells you clearly that whatever state you are in when the end comes, in that state you will remain for eternity. If you are found on the last day to be unjustified by Christ, polluted with your sin, you will bear the consequences personally and eternally. Equally, if on that day it is found Christ has redeemed you from the curse of the law and has made you the righteousness of God in him by virtue of his taking your sin and paying its penalty, then you will be found to have the necessary holiness to qualify you to see God (Hebrews 12:14). Either you will be found in Christ (Philippians 3:9) with the right to the Tree of Life (v. 14) and a passport to enter the New Jerusalem, or you will be eternally outside (v. 15) with the dogs of religious whoredom who commit spiritual fornication with every sort of deviant falsehood, with sorcerers who trust in dumb idols, and with all others who have refused to submit to the truth and righteousness of God.

Pronouncing The Call Of God

I spent a significant amount of time when I was working commuting in and out of London. At Kings Cross station, just before a train's departure you hear this announcement, "If you intend to travel on this service, please join the train now as it is ready to depart." The gospel call to repentance and faith remains open to the very end of time. In verse 10, John is told not to seal the sayings of the prophecy of this book, for the time is at hand. In other words it must be kept open to public scrutiny, it must be preached and declared. The white horse of the first seal must continue to go forth in this fallen world right up to the end.

The call that must continue to go out until the end is written in verse 17. The call is to come to Christ believing in him. The Philippian jailer asked, "What must I do to be saved?" and the answer Paul gave him is the same one that must continue to be proclaimed until Christ returns in final judgment. "Believe on the Lord Jesus Christ and thou shalt be saved." The Spirit and the bride issue the call. The Spirit filled church, comprising God's two witnesses of Revelation 11, its people and its ministers, by preaching the gospel declare salvation accomplished to all who have ears to hear; all who thirst for eternal life. And those who hear, issue the call to others to come. The preaching of the gospel is foolishness to the natural man without the quickening of God's Spirit but with his quickening, God's elect are made willing in the day of his power to believe him (Psalm 110:3).

Can you hear this final call? Look how wide open the door is, but do not wait for "the train is ready to depart". Perhaps you are concerned you do not have the right fare? Then you missed the announcement. "Whosoever will, let him take of the water of life freely." Listen to the 'conditions of carriage' as they are found in Isaiah, 'Thus saith the Lord, As the new wine is found in the cluster, and one saith, Destroy it not; for a blessing is in it: so will I do for my servants' sakes, that I may not destroy them all. And I will bring forth a seed out of Jacob, and out of Judah an inheritor of my mountains: and mine elect shall inherit it, and my servants shall dwell there' (Isaiah 65:8, 9). However unlikely looking are the objects of God's grace, there is a blessing in it, a blessing in fallen humanity by virtue of the grace of God in salvation accomplished. The blessing is pronounced in verse 14, the qualification for access to the tree of life and eligibility to pass through the gates of the celestial city is simply that we do his commandments.

Ah, but you say, I have failed to do his commandments. Indeed you have, 'for all have sinned and come short of the glory of God' (Romans 3:23). But there is good news in the gospel when Christ tells us that to do the works of God is to believe on him whom God has sent (John 6:29). The whole matter is summarised by the Apostle Paul when he says, 'Being justified freely by his grace through the redemption that is in Christ Jesus ... that he (God) might be just, and the justifier of him which believeth in Jesus ... we conclude that a man is justified by faith without the deeds of the law' (Romans 3:24-28). In his death at Calvary, Christ satisfied God's offended law and upheld the justice of God for the people given to him by the Father before time began. Faith, that is, trusting and believing in him, is what apprehends, or receives and appropriates all the blessings of salvation. I have pointed out before, it was not Abraham's believing that was counted to him for righteousness (Romans 4:3) but Christ's death to which Abraham looked forward in faith. Do you see it?

186

Do you thirst for forgiveness of sin? Well come and take of the water of life freely! Hear John 3:36, 'He that believeth on the Son hath everlasting life: and he that believeth not the Son shall not see life; but the wrath of God abideth on him.' Heed the call and come to Christ in faith to make your calling and election sure (2 Peter 1:10).

Blessing The True People Of God
Finally, we reach the final words of Revelation and of the whole Bible. This is God's word, the perfect law (James 1:25), the completed Word of God which must not be added to, or subtracted from. As the hymn, 'How Firm A Foundation' says about the scriptures, 'What more can he say than to you he hath said?' Remember how much God has exalted and guarded his Word, 'thou hast magnified thy word above all thy name' (Psalm 138:2). We need to be clear and firm to shun any notion of additional, 'charismatic' revelation from God. Everything that claims to be new revelation in addition to the completed scripture is a delusion from Satan's false prophet.

The whole of the Bible is designed by God to reveal the truth of Christ to the people of his choice in this world. Again and again, as God's Word pronounces judgment on sin it underlines the blessings of redemption on his elect. And the final verse of the Bible continues and completes that pronouncement of blessing. 'The grace of our Lord Jesus Christ be with you all, Amen.' As long as this present world continues, God's people must wait patiently, looking for, praying for, hoping for the certain return of Christ. 'Even so come Lord Jesus' (v. 20). But, all the time assured of God's undeserved, gracious blessing and favour on his people by the promise of his Word.

What a comfort! What a solid foundation for on-going, patient trust. AMEN, so shall it be.

187

Index Of Bible Verses

189

Matthew

1:21	184
2:12	106
4:8, 9	49
5:6	175
6	120
6:9-13	69
6:10	131
7:22	126
7:24	19
11:28	65, 169
11:29	155
12:29	102, 107
13:6	28
13:46	179
22:11-13	154
24:9	55
24:22	116
25:31-34	174
25:31-40	127
25:40	146
25:41	174

Mark

6:50	74
13:20	120

Luke

2:34	136
8:18	19
10:18	74
12:32	110
12:40	135
14:16-24	185
15:22	154
17:20-37	58
17:26-30	77
17:32-37	128
22:3	107
24	17
24:45	53

John

1:1	161, 184
1:14	161
1:18	155, 161
1:36	155
3:16	168
3:36	187
6:28, 29	127
6:29	105fn.,186
6:39	120

7:37, 38	175
10:9	179
10:27	123, 184
14:6	160
14:9	155, 161
16:33	110
17:5	155
17:11	90
17:15	90
17:24	152
19:30	135

Acts

2:23	102
2:42	179
13:48	124
16:14	124
17:10, 11	19
17:27, 28	35
18:28	161
20:27	17, 24, 39
26:24	58

Romans

1	75, 78, 80
1:3	166
3:23	186
3:24-28	186
3:26	23, 64, 97, 122
4:3	186
4:3-5	154
8:18	96
8:19-22	38
8:22	133, 172
8:26, 27	69
8:28	18, 23, 52, 56
8:28-32	116
8:33, 34	102, 103, 107, 169
8:36	57, 121
8:37	107
9-11	62
9:6	164
9:14-16	97
10:12-17	83
12:18	56
14:10	168
14:11	124
15:13	18

2 Timothy
1:9   36, 152, 178
2:2   19
3:1   21
3:1-5   73

Titus
1:4   153
2:13   26
3:9   27

Hebrews
1:1-3   23
1:14   73
2:9   155
2:13   173
2:16   49
4:12   161
6:13   82
7:25   36
9:12   55
9:27   135, 168
10:19, 20 36
10:29   76, 80
11   103, 173
11:10   173
12:14   185
12:22   173
12:24   55, 76, 160
13:10   55

James
1:25   187

1 Peter
1:3-5   44
1:7   179
2:5   121
2:5-9   88
2:24   178
3:15   90
5:8   110, 164

2 Peter
1:10   169, 187
2:4   165
2:5   83
3:3, 4   94
3:4   172
3:8, 9   25
3:10   172
3:13   172

1 John
2:15-17   150
2:18   116
2:22   116
3:2   175
3:13   56
4:1   24, 87
4:1-3   140, 161
4:3   116
4:17   162
5:4, 5   109

2 John
7   116

Jude
14   173

Revelation
1:1   36, 59, 112, 159
1:3   12, 68, 87, 141
1:5, 6   23
1:6   180
1:18   27
1:20   39
2:1   27
2:4   30
2:7   28, 33
2:10, 11 33
2:11   28
2:14   31
2:15   31
2:17   28, 33
2:20   31
2:24   29
2:26   28
2:26-28   33
2:27   100
2:29   28
3:1   32, 88
3:4, 5   33
3:5   28
3:6   28
3:9   55
3:12   28, 33
3:15, 16 32
3:18   33
3:19, 20 29
3:21   28, 33
4:1   36
4:2   36
4:4   63

Index Of Bible Verses

The Kingdom Of God Triumphant